Me, Myself and Paris

One Toe Under the Eiffel Tower, The Other in the Grocery Store

Me, Myself and Paris

One Toe Under the Eiffel Tower, The Other in the Grocery Store

Ruth Yunker

Cover Illustration by Ginger Triplett

Author photograph by Jeri Koegel

Outskirts Press, Inc.
Denver, Colorado

Me, Myself and Paris
One Toe Under the Eiffel Tower, The Other in the Grocery Store

Cover Illustration by Ginger Triplett
Author photograph by Jeri Koegel

Outskirts Press, Inc.
http://www.outskirtspress.com

ISBN: 978-1-4327-5714-4

Library of Congress Control Number: 2010929815

Outskirts Press and the "OP" logo are trademarks belonging to Outskirts Press, Inc.

PRINTED IN THE UNITED STATES OF AMERICA

For my mother
Margaret Frances Kaelin Yunker

I miss you every day.

Table of Contents

PARIS

Paris metamorphosed on a hot day, on the beach in Southern California. It was murky, the kind of day when the ocean air smells like fish and brings in hordes of flies. Everything looked beautiful and serene, but the citizens were sweating. This is not something Southern Californians expect to do outside the gym or menopause.

I was out under the carport, on the alley side of the house, spray-painting a twisting, gnarled piece of driftwood I'd dragged in from the beach. I was painting it sky blue. A famous English gardener had painted a dead tree of his sky blue. The effect had been amazing. So I thought, Hey! I'll do the same with my driftwood here, thereby effortlessly creating a piece of folk art to liven up the sand.

And along the way it just might liven me up.

So it was with a true sense of purpose I was out there spray-painting in the claustrophobic heat.

Spray-painting was not as easy as I thought it would be. Soon I had sky-blue paint in my hair, under my fingernails, and outlining my lips. I was grim, hot, and brooking no interference. I was determined to finish, although by now it was obvious I had seriously overestimated the importance of the project, and that actually this was a mission for a five-year-old.

Along came an elderly neighbor leaning on a cane, walking her poodle. I knew she was a neighbor because I had seen her strolling before.

This being California, where one does not talk casually to neighbors, especially if they are busy creating art in their own carport, I was startled when the old lady paused. She perused my work, oblivious to her poorly timed intrusion. I even politely stopped painting, waiting to see what she had to say. I puffed up a little in readiness for her compliment.

Finally she spoke. "Ah," she said. "You're doing crafts, my dear. How very nice."

Crafts? Nice?

She tottered away before I could grab her scrawny throat, kicking away the cane as I did so, pretending I was aiming for the dog. But then she might have claimed elder abuse. Old ladies know their rights.

I watched her tiny rear teeter complacently away and was filled with venom…which quickly segued into horror.

Crafts? I looked to this old woman like I was engaged in crafts?

Was this a metaphor for my whole life at this point? Was this how I came across? A middle-aged woman, children all grown, at a total loss as to how to fill her time? I was sullen and disheveled. Sweating sky-blue paint. And I'd just been reduced to…crafts.

Shoot me now—

But then a moment of clarity—

The old hag was right. I *was* in murky shape. I was listless, no direction solid enough to be called a direction. Certainly no plan. Nothing new and different, no challenge looming in my future.

I'd been telling myself I was just getting over some family things. I'd divorced my husband. It had been my idea… but nonetheless—

My mother had died…a hole that could never be filled.

But time had passed. Enough time. Even my children were on the right track at last.

My heart started to race, just a little. I eyed the wet blue driftwood.

It was time to do something different. Time to—

Get out of town…way the hell out of town.

Just like that?

Yes.

I felt a…was that an excited flutter? My ears tingled. Maybe it was the spray paint? Causing caustic poisoning?

Get out of town! Oh, the sweeping vistas surrounding those words—

Because I believe totally in the restorative powers of leaving town.

I dragged the wet driftwood to its spot out on the beach, my mind already on a plane—

Okay, so, I would go alone. Yes. That's what I needed. Alone time.

And I would go for a whole year.

YES!

Such was my thinking as I threw the sky-blue driftwood up against the palm out front, where it grabbed hold, a spindly praying mantis, looking like it was about to climb to the top.

Not folk art, no. But still, it did have a certain fey quality, a certain joie de vivre—

I wanted some joie de vivre.

I stalked back into the house to plan my escape.

I didn't hit on Paris right away. I hit on Florence. But Florence is in Italy, and I didn't speak a word of Italian—

I'd worry about that later.

I couldn't go for a year, either. Who was I kidding? Besides domestic duties, how did I plan to afford an entire year away? I'm not the five-dollar-a-day sort, and well past the age where sleeping in hostels could have been a viable solution.

Six weeks? Six weeks was good. Longer than a month, which gave the enterprise a more risqué, self-indulgent tone. A good thing.

I would rent an apartment, for that complete immersion. I'd have no hotel at my back. No busy thoroughfare. No, I'd stay in a neighborhood somewhere. Live like a native, see.

So, where?

I'd lived in Brussels, Belgium when I was a teenager. I had been totally angry about it at the time. There was to be no American high school experience for me. No Ann-Margret in *Bye Bye Birdie*. No cheerleading. No football-playing boyfriend. No American clothes and music—

What I did get was a lot of travel, which I loved, for the most part. It was sunny every time I was taken to London. I adored Rome. Athens and I were meant to be. In Lisbon I danced with a seventeen-year-old roué who told me I was the most beautiful girl he'd ever met, and I believed him.

I'd never been to Florence—

I began to waiver when I contemplated Italian, of which I knew none. If I were to stash myself in a neighborhood, wouldn't it be helpful to speak even a bit of the language?

I'd learned to speak French in Brussels...

I knew where this was going. Paris should seriously be considered. The language thing was important, and I knew it—

But I hadn't liked Paris when I was dragged there, age

thirteen. As far as I was concerned it was nothing but a bigger, dirtier Brussels.

I'd whined audibly in front of the Mona Lisa (so small and dirty), and what was up with that walk to even get to it. Obviously the Louvre suffered from illusions of grandeur.

I'd refused to climb to the top of the Eiffel Tower, and furthermore agreed with the original detractors that it was hideous, and even more damning, silly.

And no, I didn't think the view from our hotel rooms of l'Opera Garnier was sublime. If it wasn't the skyscrapers of New York City, then I was in the wrong life.

But now...Paris was the best I could come up with to blow some fresh air into my very soul?

Besides, going to Paris was a cliché. Everyone loved and adored Paris. Why didn't I get really brave and go for Istanbul or Stockholm or even Morocco?

Moxy. Go get some.

But the practical kept returning me squarely to Paris. What was my problem anyway? I'd just given myself six weeks away. Such a time away wouldn't be all peaches and cream. But knowing a little of the language would help... and I knew it. Even though I hadn't spoken French in years, I was pretty certain there would be enough to creep up from the depths and present me with a phrase here and there, just in the nick of time. Like as the metro doorways are closing and I finally understand the shouted message floating in my direction. "Wrong metro, Madame—"

I heaved a sigh, caved to practicality, and chose Paris.

What one has to do to grow, you know? What one has to do to rise to the challenge.

So, I settled on Paris. I went for six weeks. In October and November.

I went again the next year.

And the next year as well.

Because, it happened to me. Just like with everyone else. I fell totally and irrevocably in love with Paris.

All because that old woman with her poodle spoke the truth when she could have simply minded her own business.

JACQUES' INSTRUCTIONS

I oozed sixteen hours of airplane ozone. My suitcases were dead walruses at my feet. I'd finally made it through customs, been driven from the airport by an enthusiastic driver who had just spent two years in New York. He'd been more than happy to practice his English on me.

We found the apartment building, which turned out to be in the farther reaches of the Marais, in what was a predominantly Asian neighborhood. The door was a magnificent red, but was covered with graffiti. French graffiti, which gave it a lyrical quality to my bleary eyes.

And then we'd waited for what seemed forever for Jacques to appear. Jacques being the landlord's right-hand man, and boyfriend, as it turned out.

He did show up, at a run, tucking his spotless shirt into good jeans. Of course he was ridiculously good-looking, as had been the young driver. Whose hand I now shook in fervent gratitude for getting me this close, oh so close, to my destination.

Then Jacques shook my hand with apparent enthusiasm, and led me down a dark passageway to the ground-floor apartment.

The building was five floors tall, and plastic sheeting

hung from the roof to my door. "Terribly sorry about zees. Just a little work needs to be done on zee building. Paris law," he said, shrugging, smiling ruefully. I was beyond caring. There's the door, buster. Open it up and leave me alone.

He swung the doors open, ripped at least three ligaments hoisting my bags in—

And then, somehow I just thought, you know, he'd leave. Leave me to myself at this blissful moment…like they do in hotels.

Non.

This was not a hotel. This was a real live apartment. And as such, there would be certain domestic details about which I needed to know. And Jacques here was going to tell me all about it.

I was licked. I knew it, so I clung to the back of a chair and fluttered a hand.

Jacques began and, before my eyes, became a thudding bulldog with zee domestic details. He licked his chops, and a torrent of instructions began.

"Just two codes for the door, Madame. It is easy, yes?"

Two codes? How about no codes? I hate codes. Where did it say anything about codes? But even in a jetlagged fog, I understood that precision was a must when it came to the codes. I fumbled through my purse and found a pen. "Write them down," I said. Maybe I said please.

Next came the keys. Okay. I could do keys. Jacques dangled them in front of me. But he made this complicated too. There was only one key, but he'd made two copies of it in different shades of copper. Sweat dripped off my upper lip.

Now he led me to the washer and dryer. Was he kidding? Did I look like the kind of woman who needed to be told how to work a washing machine? Especially now, two minutes off a twelve-hour flight? He had to be kidding, right?

He wasn't kidding. Well, I wouldn't listen to these instructions. I knew how to operate a goddamn washing machine, okay?

After a bit, I said, *"C'est tout?"* Politely. Cautiously. I wanted Jacques out of the apartment so I could make it mine. So I could be free to be me. So I could start my goddamn six weeks, okay?

My wish was a non-happening. As if attention to domestic details could ever be underestimated.

And it was obvious he was on a mission. His boyfriend must have told him he could not return until the American woman in the ground-floor apartment knew everything there was to know, so that she would not bother them later with endless questions.

So, the workings of the washer and dryer were followed by showing me the bathroom. Which could only be reached by mincing sideways, on tiptoe, down a tiny flight of stairs.

The bathroom itself had been carved out of subterranean Paris. God knew what lurked on the other side of those walls.

However, the bathroom itself, tiny to the max, was modern and bright. Orange, yellow, and white tile. Like sunshine. Okay. I like sunshine below sea level. There was a chic washbasin. I liked that too.

But then Jacques swept open the shower curtains, and I beheld a handheld shower hose. At the sight of that hose, what that meant to my daily shower sank in, and I now noticed that my shoulders, already hunched up around my ears, were still set in the shape of the airplane seat.

Back up on the surface Jacques smiled, a sweet smile.

"So, all is easy, yes? The washer and dryer?"

"Yes."

"The bathroom?"

Don't remind me.

"The codes?"

My eyes made a desperate sweep of the numbers written down. The page was upside down. "Yes."

Finally, reluctantly, his eyes still casting about for further issues, he shrugged, eyed me appraisingly.

I clutched my hands.

It was silent—

A small sigh, a brief purse of his lips, and finally, finally, he left, closing the heavy door with care.

I looked around, scarcely believing I was alone at last. It was only then I saw the apartment was a tiny jewel. Golden wood floors, white upon white bed linens, wrought-iron chairs, the latest coffeemaker, and a white and gold vase filled with stargazer lilies set on the miniscule dining table. It was perfect.

Yes!

BAGGING MY GROCERIES

My small stash of groceries sat in a jumble at the end of the checkout counter, no one rushing forward to bag them. I had no idea why my little stash of groceries—Gruyere, eggs, cookies, milk, and Kleenex—just sat there at the end of the counter like that. The blasé cashier handed me my change. There was a silence. Even the man who'd been talking the cashier's ear off shut up.

What? What came next?

I was just off the plane, for godsake. Couldn't she tell? I was Californian to boot. We are not a subtle people. Don't even Parisians know this? I needed to be told what to do here. What the hell did she want me to do? I honestly didn't have a clue. I probably wouldn't have been able to tie my shoe at this point either, so maybe it really was jet lag keeping me in the dark.

The cashier eyed me. She came to a conclusion—

She reached to a rack of plastic bags, right by my pile of waiting groceries, pulled one off, shook it out, and tried to hand it to me.

I looked at the plastic bag, now on hyper alert. What did she want? Was she asking me if this was the kind of bag I wanted? Paper or plastic? All that?

I could hardly stand it. I'd just paid, for godsake. Wasn't that good enough? That I'd paid in euros and all, and hadn't stood there in front of her weeping, pathetically offering her a ten-dollar bill, claiming tourist's dispensation?

Wasn't it enough that I had actually remembered I needed milk for my coffee? Couldn't she tell I'd already lowered my personal standards by going into a Starbucks to buy a bag of French Roast, because even though I intended to live like a native (who did a tad of sightseeing on the side), I just wasn't up to messing with my daily morning libation? And that my French had not risen to the challenge at Starbucks, as to how to tell the kid taking the order which type of grind I needed, and a veritable Charades had been needed just to make it happen?

And that even now, here at this tiny corner grocery, I'd only bought the extra things to practice, and maybe I should have gone straight back to the teeny apartment and to bed in those gorgeous white sheets, and dealt with the milk for my coffee in the morning, when at least it would be light outside, and I could see just exactly how run down this particular part of Paris actually was—

And that even now, I was none too sure how to get home, although the sight of the moon hanging over the Seine was enough to make it all worthwhile. I'd even ordered and eaten a Nutella crepe. And was damn proud of that too. So why the hang-up now—

What did this blond chick with the ponytail want? And what was with that ponytail? Was she an Orange County wannabe?

She rattled the bag at me sharply. More loud silence.

And suddenly I got it. I was supposed to pack my own groceries.

I panicked. I was still in the process of fumbling my euros back into my wallet. A coin dropped to the floor. A bill stuck to the outside of the wallet rather than sliding in. The plastic bag now dangled from my pinkie.

The girl turned away from me and recommenced her conversation with the man, who seemed to have just decided to never bag another grocery. What did I know. They didn't leap to help. What they did do, I realized later, was politely look away and pretend they weren't noticing I was about to collapse in nervous hysteria.

Actually grateful for this, and really really grateful there was no one in line behind me, I packed my things. It took two plastic bags, which required the dexterity of a robot to open. Then I glanced down on the ground for the coin. No coin in sight, of course. To hell with it. I picked up my purse and the two bags. I couldn't manage a polite good-bye, let alone a *merci*…for what, anyway?

I finally got out of there. The cool air felt good on my red face. The sidewalk was dirty. Maybe I still hate Paris?

The man from inside the store hurried out after me. "Madame?"

I turned. He handed me my coin—

Okay, maybe I don't hate Paris.

CLIMBING
THE NOTRE DAME

My boots were chocolate suede. They had toes sharp enough to slice tomatoes. I'd brought them so I'd have something chic for my feet. But it was turning out that I walked ten million miles a day, so the gorgeous boots had been sitting in my closet. Until today, when essentially I dared myself to wear them. Parisian women could handle these masochistic boots. They trudged millions of miles on a daily basis too. I'd been in Paris a week and a half now. It was time for the next step.

It was 3:30 in the afternoon. I'd just gorged on duck salad, poached egg, and a huge amount of butter.

Suddenly there was the Notre Dame, looming, stately, surrounded by people and pigeons and a vitality that spoke to its place in history. And right in front of it, up front and personal, was a sign so small I don't know how I even saw it. The beyond miniscule sign pointed the way to the roof.

I've climbed to the top of tall tourist traps. So I knew better. But my dutiful inner tourist leapt up, and I found myself following the sign. Just to see. No commitment. I knew better, right? Don't forget the boots—

But that malicious cretin, my inner tourist, led me to a small side door beckoningly oh so seductively. I had the correct euros. But I knew better, right? I really did know better—

I got in line.

And one second later, fifty other innocents and I were herded through a small arch in a thick stone wall, and without so much as a breath of pity from the hired help, the climb began. And from the very first step, I knew I had made a monumental error. Memories of other tourist climbs I'd made flashed before my eyes—

I panicked.

I tried to turn back…

I would apologize profusely, and not ask for my money back.

But…I couldn't turn back. There were a million people behind me. There were a million people in front of me, too, although this actually translated into a single pair of black Mephistos ascending the steep and narrow and claustrophobic stone steps in front of me. I was trapped. I was a woman in a black hole, a cavern of death.

No way out. In pitiless boots.

Survival mode raised its weak hand. Don't panic, I said sternly to myself, as if talking thusly would encourage me to believe I was on a stroll in the park. Do not get claustrophobic. Whatever you do, do not get claustrophobic.

I can't breathe—

Think wide open. Top of mountain. Focus, for godsake.

I focused on the black shoes climbing up in front of me—

I did not focus on how narrow the circular stairs were. I did not focus on how there couldn't possibly be enough air to go around. I did not allow for the possibility of fainting, although the idea had great appeal.

But no. No idiocy. I could do this—

No I couldn't. No I wouldn't.

Yes I could. I was a big girl. Hell, I was a grown woman.

Who should have known better.

I was panting. Already I'm panting?

Don't think, for chrissake—

Don't swear. This is a cathedral. Is such a word appropriate in here?

In here? This was hell in here. Gimme a break. This was a nightmare. A total nightmare.

Up, up, up, narrow little stone steps, surrounded front and back. This was a torture chamber. Why did the stairs circle like this? This church wasn't big enough for a sweeping flight of stairs? Complete with landings, and maybe even stretchers? How about mirrors to give the illusion of space, even though there wasn't any. Could this stairwell have been made any smaller?

My toes were now numb. I was trudging, shaky, on the verge of maniacal screaming. My thighs burned. I couldn't breathe.

I clumped and clumped, because there was no stopping. Anxiety attack clawing to be let loose.

I was claustrophobic. Ever since I did acupuncture that one year. Thank you, acupuncture—

I was out of shape. Hadn't done any exercise since I twisted my hip or whatever I'd done, in yoga. Thank you, yoga.

And don't forget that lunch. Duck. God, how I hate duck.

Okay, shut up. Breathe. Okay, pant then. Whatever. Keep going—

I *am* going…like I have any choice—

This will end…won't it?

Maybe I'd actually have a heart attack, right here, right now. I was no longer too young for such a possibility. Didn't my father have one at my age?

Maybe I'd just throw up, going around in circles like this.

Did the people who built this torture chamber run around in circles for fun? This spiral up, this strangulated ode to the twist. It couldn't have been to save room. Yeah right. Har, har. Save room in this monstrous pile of rocks? Space was at a premium in the Notre Dame? C'mon, the devil made them do it. It's so obvious.

God, like for how long had we been climbing, climbing, climbing? Fifteen minutes? A half hour? Ten years?

How could I have forgotten that hideous climb up to the roof of Saint Peter's? I was only twelve, but it almost did me in. Hadn't I promised I'd never climb anything again? And the next day when we were at the Sistine Chapel, didn't I scream when it was suggested we climb up to the top of that?

But I remembered now. It was horrible climbing up to the top of Saint Peter's. I was sure that I'd gotten lost because I climbed, like, forever. But I was also sure I wasn't lost because again, it had been a narrow space with no deviation from the direction of up, up, up those curving stone steps—

Why are they always so narrow?

Why don't these cathedral people get a life and install elevators? Banks of elevators. All over the place. Right by the front door. Huge commercial elevators. They'd fit right in with the beggar woman outside the front door, her cup a torn-off Starbucks cup.

I hate elevators.

Never mind.

At Saint Peter's I'd been all alone. No sweaty bodies in front of me or behind me. Was that possible? I certainly wasn't alone up on the roof of Saint Peter's. It was a regular shopping mall up there, I found. Kiosks all over the place. I was shocked. I was twelve, prim, Catholic. Shocked to see commercialism up there on the roof of Saint Peter's.

I was also upset. There were gorgeous rosaries up there, and I had no money with me.

I've heard the kiosks aren't there anymore.

It was cold, that time in Rome, when I was twelve.

It was not cold now.

It was hot. It was five thousand degrees Fahrenheit in here. We were trapped in here. We'd died and gone to hell.

So hell turned out to be this…climbing round and round, up a stony stairwell in an immense edifice, caught between hysteria and terror, night sweats and hangovers, between guardrails and the endless plunge.

I was going to faint.

I didn't care if I fainted—

Please God, make me faint.

I couldn't go another step.

I wouldn't go another step—

And then…then a shadow of something filtered down through the feet in front of me. It seemed to be light. A lightness of spirit. Hope?

Hope traveled down the line, getting to me finally. The

collective hope of fifty people trapped climbing in a stairwell built just too long ago to have any relevance anymore. Hope dispelling despair, because, yes—

It was getting lighter.

The air began to thin out ahead of me. I couldn't see it. Just an inkling was all. But this inkling was enough.

I stared at the black shoes in front of me, always two steps ahead of me, going to get there before me no matter what. Finally I was in love with those black shoes, which had suffered the same agonies I had--

When suddenly the shoes disappeared. I reached out desperately. Don't leave me.

And then my eyes were no longer staring at the next stone step in front of me.

My eyes came into contact with the bright blue outdoors, or in this case, the bright gray outdoors, as I climbed up those last few stone steps and wobbled out onto the roof of the Notre Dame de Paris—

Breathing deep, hungry gasps of freedom.

The people who immediately rush to the edge of infinity and throw themselves over the railing to stare at the view amaze me. They dive into it like God is personally hanging onto the seat of their pants. I admire their trust that precautions are in place. I applaud their rock-solid knees.

I can't do it.

The minute we made it to the roof of the Notre Dame, memory of the climb left like it had never happened. Vertigo swept it.

As usual I was surprised. I love roller coasters. I love the Alps and the High Sierra Nevadas. What is this fear of heights thing? It attacks without warning…like every time I ascend tall places, and sometimes in the middle of driving over a bridge, like that time over the Chesapeake Bay. This gets on my nerves. This shows no savoir-faire whatsoever.

But so, I had to hang back. I hung onto the walls, lurking back in the shadows, as my fellow climbers swooped to the edge like hawks. I hoped I seemed to be casually letting everyone else have their day at the guardrails, staring hungrily down, down, down at the ground so very far away, when of course, I couldn't move. My knees didn't work. I was praying that my legs wouldn't give way completely, and that the ground under my feet would stop pitching, stop trying to throw me off the roof.

Is this any way to travel? This is why I hate sightseeing. One is just not completely in control of any situation.

After a bit, I was able to glance around very carefully. If I didn't swing my head it seemed I was okay. So I inched to the railing and peered out, straight ahead, straight out at the rooftops of Paris (which are famous in their own right, okay, so worth climbing to the roof of the Notre Dame for an extra special view of them), careful to look nowhere at anything that looked like the ground.

The rooftops looked just like all those photos one sees all the time. I'd seen pictures. Charming as all get-out.

So I began to gaze about me, way up high on the Notre Dame. And my eyes finally zeroed in on what was up there right in front of me.

I finally saw creatures made of stone, perched on the walls, laughing and making fun of the tourists, and gazing out over their very own Paris, alive with insouciance and fun, possessing a wit that obviously could be wicked and quick, not suffering fools gladly—

I saw the chimeras. I fell in love with the chimeras.

It was their world up there in the wind, overlooking all of Paris.

I'd seen them in pictures before, and gargoyles too. It turned out that gargoyles are rainspouts, clinging to the sides of buildings. Chimeras are not waterspouts.

They were having a gala up there. They were happy, indeed complacently happy, and superior. Even the one who appeared to be eating a small cat. They stared out over Paris with the highest of amusement. I could almost hear their sardonic comments, aimed at the human race in general, the mindless rush of humanity below, the muddle of the rest of the world. They escaped all that up here.

It was a windblown existence, yes, and cold, certainly the day I was there, but crouched up on the walls, hunkered amidst the stone, age and history permeating the air they were inhaling, munching and gnawing on their toys, it was perfection. They gazed down on Paris with bellies of laughter.

They were skinny and hunched, but now that I saw them up close, they had obviously held opinions, and seemed like they'd be able to rise to the level of polite candor if needed. They exuded such a sense of knowingness.

A German boy stood next to me. He was about twenty. I was so filled with happiness by these chimeras, I had to tell someone. So first I practiced the French in my head. Then I said to him, "They look so happy, the chimeras. I'm surprised."

He looked surprised I was talking to him. But then he swept a happy gaze at the closest ones to us. "Yes, they are happy looking at Paris all below." I could hear the German accent in his French.

The wind blew. It was overcast, but I could see the Sacre Coeur on the crest above Montmartre. Everyone was photographing the chimeras. They sat there in total acceptance of our fascination, like rock stars. Like sardonic comics.

Like sages, too. Which comes from living up in the windy skies of Paris, in the medieval stone of the Notre Dame.

EYE CONTACT

Parisians do not make eye contact. Eye contact is considered gauche, even rude. Not for the Parisian to look happy out on the sidewalks. God forbid even a touch of goodwill lights up their Gallic features, lightens up those serious hearts. For it is indeed a serious business being Parisian.

Being a Californian, I don't do sidewalks. So that finding myself actually out on sidewalks, my suddenly endangered body not protected by a car, was hugely disorienting and disconcerting. I tried to tell myself it was exotic…it's not. Occasionally I looked to a stranger with whom I could exchange a quick smile of recognition at the humor and danger of actually being afoot on a real live street.

Forget it.

But one time I needed a smile. It was my first trip. And it had been a long afternoon.

I had, with great difficulty, solved a financial crisis. I needed to break a five-hundred-euro bill into smaller, more acceptable bills. It had taken four banks, three credit unions, and two tries at the same place before I landed, trembling and weary, in front of one totally dour matron. But this matron did, after considerable pursing of her lips, take pity on me, and give me smaller euros.

I slobbered my thanks all over her solid hand and inched out the door backwards. I vowed to myself that I would brave the ATM machine for my next dose of cash. I told myself that the nice French banks would not eat my card, but I didn't believe that for one second—

Issues involving money were mountains at this point in my adjustment to Paris.

Out on the sidewalk, I wanted…no, I *needed* a smile.

I decided to throw good manners to the wind. I *would* get my smile.

I paused out there in the middle of the rushing sidewalk, and zeroed in on the trillions of French faces coming at me, going around me. Scarves. Umbrellas. Trench coats. No one looked at me. No one would catch my eye. But I was determined. I slowed to a crawl and scanned the crowds.

Finally there she was. An intelligent-looking woman my age. She wore a belted coat like mine. I liked her shoes. She'd like mine, I knew, if we were ever introduced properly. She could do it. She could manage a smile for a needy stranger. Her defenses were probably down, anyway. She was probably focusing on something like what to make for dinner. She'd smile before she knew what hit her.

She and I drew closer.

I saw her glance at my coat. Ah good. We may as well have been sisters. So I zeroed in for the kill. I took a breath and smiled full on at her. It was a blinding Southern Californian kind of a smile. I threw in the force of friendliness I never feel at home. I briefly thought of the many neighbors who would not have recognized me, such was the bonhomie suffusing my person.

But, oh no. A smile did not automatically flash onto her face, as it would have done at home.

No. She saw the smile, and immediately her face collapsed into consternation. As we drew closer still, her look changed to one of pure horror because of the most embarrassing issue that even though I seemed to know her, she did not recognize me. She clutched tightly onto her purse. In one second this woman turned from a vision of calm determination to one of hunkering discombobulation.

I was immediately beyond embarrassed. My intention had not been to mortify the woman.

Yes, I'd felt fragile, in need of a friendly face. But this was not America, where friendly faces are a dime a dozen. This was Paris, where friendly faces seemed to be nonexistent, particularly on the sidewalk, rushing home after a hard day's work.

I cringed.

I have no idea how the woman coped with the appalling moment when we actually passed each other, for I was doing my best to regain even a modicum of the polite Parisian, and was now staring diligently across the street at a window display of naked male mannequins painted silver.

However, to give and receive a smile is a holistically approved action. Even if the French were willfully ignoring the dictates of edifying behavior, did this mean I should adversely affect my own well-being?

I took to smiling at babies, in strollers at ground level, the kind who clenched a pacifier between their teeth. I hoped to see a wobbly lift of the lips on either side of the pacifier before they realized what they were doing. I didn't want any trouble from the parents, a high-strung segment of the population in the first place.

Some babies actually smiled back outright, dropping the pacifier. Lovely.

But other babies? Their Parisian parents had gotten to them first.

It was tough, but eventually as with all difficulties in life, I acclimated, and no eye contact got easier. Smiling at strangers began to seem a waste of facial muscle power, in fact pointless.

One time though, I was standing waiting for the metro. I was minding my own business, listening to the echoes of the "Maple Leaf Rag" being played on an accordion just around the corner. I was thinking about Josephine Baker, and wondering if Fats Waller had ever gotten to Paris, and thanking God for the Internet because I would know the answer the minute I got back to the apartment.

A train going in the opposite direction pulled in.

Inside the lighted car sat a little boy, talking and laughing to himself, his fingers drawing imaginary creatures on the window. I smiled at the sight of him in spite of myself.

He saw me. His hands stopped moving. So I smiled again. I threw in a discreet little wave of my hand. His mouth dropped open in surprise. He grinned. He dropped his eyes shyly, then looked again. So, tossing caution to the wind, I waved again. Warmth suffused my temporary Parisian soul.

Then he threw himself back in his seat, and looked happily up at his mother seated opposite.

I'd forgotten about Maman.

I cast a quick look at her—

She sat stark upright, staring at me, her eyes bullets. She held her large purse like a bazooka. It was aimed straight at me.

Inside my tailored coat and expertly wrapped scarf, I shrank. I became a woman of suspect moral character of the lowest kind, right there in the metro station of Alma Marceau.

The train pulled out. I did not wave to the little boy. I did not meet Maman's ferocious gaze.

That night I made myself go to a poetry reading at the Red Wheelbarrow, a quaint and crowded English bookstore in Le Marais. I knew I'd find Americans there. The kind who smile at strangers. I'd smile back.

Hell, I'd hug.

THE QUINCE TART

I pushed open the door to the boulangerie, and the warm, sweet scent of baked pastries sent me to heaven. Boulangeries are cocoons. Like sweet kitchens. Like Christmas cards from olden days. The scents enveloped me. I was starved. I wanted a nice little superlative French pastry snack. This snack was to last me my walk from here in Le Marias to the Notre Dame just over on the Île de la Cité, where I intended to photograph the pigeons and a man who fed them.

I'd picked up on how to stop for a quick pastry at one of the millions of boulangeries in Paris. The choices were dizzying, or pure and simple, because each and every butter croissant, loaf of sugar bread, bacon and cheese quiche, plain brioche, and on and on, was perfection. It didn't matter which one I chose. All were equally fantastic—

Except for *the* one, that is. The one that rose above all the rest. The one that deserves a place in history—

The almond croissant from the Bon Marche. Oh my, yes.

This croissant was a duchess. It was so indolent with elegance, so rich and so saturated with butter, so laden with almond paste conjuring up the Ottoman Empire, so heavy to be held, it had to be eaten over the course of two days.

In honor of its sensual aura, I lit candles. I set the table as if preparing for a four- course meal. I used the linen napkins. I ate with knife and fork.

I gave it my full attention, to honor the exquisite sweetness of the almond, the delicate but crisp croissant itself oh so delicate. There was no reading or watching television or walking while eating this croissant—

It melted in my mouth, its flavor, the texture, and the aroma lighting up my world.

I could have worn the almond croissant from the Bon Marche around my neck like a medieval jewel.

It was a gray day. I was a little cold, as well as hungry. I felt acclimated enough to be fast in the boulangerie, to show I'd been around for a while, that I knew a thing or two about being quick on my feet and knowing exactly what I wanted, like the natives.

No awestruck touristy browsing for me, even though underneath my cool (right?) exterior, I was agog with delight.

I didn't want my usual apricot and cream tart that day, although they were to die for as well. *Non.* It was time to try something new, something daring.

My eyes fell on one of the huge platters upon which sat one slice. All the others were gone. I immediately deduced this must be a favorite tart. So I leaned in to see if I could read the French calligraphy which would clue me in. It took a moment, but I got it. It was a pear and quince tart.

I had no fear of quince. Actually I'd never had quince. Pear was only okay, in no way mind-boggling. In fact the tart sounded like Thanksgiving—

"Madame?"

I stood to attention. Mustn't lose face. Must know what I want. No patience was ever shown for those bumblers who didn't know what they wanted. I pointed. I paid. I was out-side with the most popular tart in Paris before I remembered how soul satisfying the apricot and cream tart always was.

But okay. I had this quince and pear tart here...even though I wasn't the biggest fan of pears. Maybe the quince would make up for the pear? But of course the quince would make up for the pear. This had been the last slice after all. Many, many others before me had chosen the pear and quince tart.

I set off for the Notre Dame. No need to look for a bench in Le Marais. There is a dearth of the ever-present green benches (upon which, at this point, I couldn't even sit) in Le Marais, where Rue de Rivoli meets Rue S. Antoine.

And I'd learned to eat while walking, which is very Parisian. So voila!

I turned immediately down a narrow street. It was called Rue du Petit Musique. Inwardly I cooed at the pretty name, ignored the dour street, and took a bite of the quince and pear tart.

My lip quivered. Something mildly...blag? A bit sickly blag? Maybe it was because I was walking while eating.

I took another bite...not so good. But this wasn't pos-sible. Certainly a tart this popular tasted fantastic, and I just wasn't used to the...er...taste.

I hadn't slept well last night either. Lack of sleep could always cause problems.

I took another bite, determined but now, also tentative. How could I not be loving a Parisian tart, especially this de-sired pear and quince thing?

I chewed, a certain queasiness now appearing. Still I chewed. No Ugly American for me. I knew how to adapt. When I was twelve and we moved to Brussels, I learned to like big, thick, ghastly bread. I learned to love something pseudo chocolate(ish)-tasting called Nutella, spread all over it. If I could do that, a small piece of tart was a cinch.

But as I chewed, the scent of the tart weaseled its way up into my nostrils. They flared in shock and I gagged.

I took a good look at the tart. Was that a...putrid odor? But in and of itself, quince was such an innocuous flavor. How could it smell bad?

But now I noticed an odd aftertaste. Kind of like moldy cat—

Was I sure? Rue du Petit Musique was a damp little street, in spite of many window boxes of geraniums. A drab little street, despite its melodious name. Maybe Rue du Petit Musique itself was what I was smelling?

I was loath to judge the quince so harshly. Was I sure this quince thing tasted like mangy cat? When was the last time I'd eaten cat?

I took another bite—

Ugh. God. Patooey.

It was horrible. Even disguised as it was by a buttery pastry, sugar, and thick cream, and the obviously superfluous pears, the flavor penetrated. And that smell hit me right to the marrow of my nostrils, the roof of my mouth. Maybe even infiltrating my joints, my ligaments—

Was this tart dangerous?

A wave of fear overtook me there on the Rue du Petit Musique. I didn't have a clue how to deal with Parisian hospitals, or, for that matter, how fast quince killed, but I knew, I just knew, it wouldn't be pretty. Either the hospital or death by quince.

I looked around for the green trash bags that hung from every other tree or lamppost. Not so on Rue du Petit

Musique. No green trash bags whatsoever. So, half running, half trotting, I ended up carrying the loathsome quince and pear carcass, without benefit of a napkin, all the way to the Notre Dame.

Where, under the amused gaze of the gargoyles, I slam-dunked it into the first green trash bag I saw.

CONVERSATION
WITH A TOURIST

In a watery sunlight, but otherwise warm day, I stood staring at a large metro map. I wasn't lost. I was staring to see if the map was starting to make sense.

And it was. Because I now saw it wasn't the metro map at all. It was the bus map, which should have been clear from the start, because it was right by a bus stop.

"Do you need help?"

I turned. An American girl in her early twenties, wearing a knapsack, slouched behind me. "No," I said, startled and irritated to be startled. "I'm just checking it out."

"Those are bus routes. I walk everywhere. I'm heading in the general direction of the Eiffel Tower. My friend's apartment where I'm staying is over there. Thank god you can see that thing from everywhere in Paris. I can always find my way back." Her tone was blasé, with a tinge of annoyance thrown in.

"You don't like the Eiffel Tower?"

"God. The Eiffel Tower is getting on my nerves. You'll see."

She could tell I was new in town? "You're not having a good time," I said just to be polite to a fellow American.

"God no. I was supposed to be in Barcelona by now. I've been stuck here for three days. It sucks."

"Sucks?" This chick was an idiot.

"I missed my flight in Iceland. Iceland was really boring, by the way. But so, I missed my flight here in Paris, and now I'm stuck till I can leave again."

I morphed into Pollyanna. "Well, I'm loving it here. I'm here for six weeks by myself, and it's all so cool to me, and everything is so beautiful and—"

"You're here for six godforsaken weeks?"

"Yes," I squealed. I couldn't seem to help myself. The girl was right. One *could* see the Eiffel Tower from just about everywhere. Using it to find your way home? How totally fab was that?

"You oughta go someplace cool like Barcelona."

"Barcelona?"

"Yeah. I'm going to Barcelona for culinary school."

The hair on my neck sprang to attention. The sullen American brat blurred. "Culinary school? You think I'd like culinary school? Let me tell you, missy, the last thing in the world I'd like is culinary school, okay? I've been cooking three meals a day for thirty-five years, and let me tell you it is one big fat goddamn drag, okay? Cooking school? You gotta be kidding."

My vision cleared. The girl was slinking away. "You don't have to be so rude," she muttered over her shoulder as she rambled off. I saw her check for the Eiffel Tower—

God, how cool was that?

I returned to perusing the bus routes map.

QUAI de la MÉGISSERIE

There is a block along the Seine, Quai de la Mégisserie, that features a pet store, then a flower shop, then another pet store, then a flower shop—repeat this maybe once more—all huddled right next to each other.

It is a mood killer, let me tell you.

I was walking home late one afternoon, very soon after my arrival, on what was turning out to be a long haul along the Seine, pretty sure I was going in the right direction, but not absolutely sure. So therefore, while dutifully gawking in wonder, I was also praying. Which was helped by stopping at an old church along the way, inside of which I swore I heard shrieks from the Lost Souls in purgatory. Of course they couldn't have been shrieks from the Great Beyond, but such was my mood, I hoped they were. I mean, hey, I was inside a very old, dark, and damp medieval church, so they could have been—

However, of course they weren't shrieks from the Lost Souls in purgatory.

Upon stepping back outside, I saw that I was right next to a school, and from behind the high walls came the shrieks of trillions of Parisian schoolchildren outside for recess.

Resolutely I continued on my way. I crossed the street, an

accomplishment in and of itself, and I was suddenly knocked flat by the odor of…a pet store? No, it couldn't be. Not here in the middle of Paris. Who wants to see a pet store in the middle of Paris? Pet stores belong in malls, out of the way, out of sight.

But yes, it was pet store, right across from the charismatic, pewter-colored Seine, right amidst the hustle and bustle of the no-nonsense Parisian crowd engrossed in their late afternoon mad dash home.

I hate pet stores.

But here it was, its heavy odor of doggie kibble, unhappy baby mill puppies, and used kitty litter, hanging in the air.

I walked hastily by—

Right next door, though, spilling its fragrant wares out onto the sidewalk, was a plant shop. The scent of stargazer lilies permeated the air. Now this was more like it—

But not quite. No. The pet store smell was doing battle. Lily and doggie aromas mingled.

It was a nose-wrinkling, toe-curling type of smell. Uncouth. Misplaced. Mood deflator.

It had been a long day. I'd ridden the metro for the first time, and whereas eventually riding the metro became second nature, that day it was a huge, knuckle-biting triumph. Which totally took the fight out of me for the rest of the day. I chose to walk home, ultimately, following the Seine. Metros are, after all, underground, and particularly claustrophobic when one is new at the game.

So that when after the plant store came another pet store—same fluorescent lighting, same smell—I thought I'd gotten turned around.

But no. It was, indeed, a second pet store. Which was followed by another plant store and more stargazer aroma mixed with puppy sweat, then another pet store, then another, yes, plant store.

I surrendered. I had to accept this perverse oddity, this assault to the nostrils. I had to turn the other cheek and pretend Paris was as flawless as I demanded it be.

I would have to let this glitch pass.

And as I did so, the Place du Châtelet appeared. This was home turf. I'd made it.

Pink with triumph, but dizzy from the smell of Fido and stargazer lily, I took the first seat I saw at the first café I came to and, without taking enough time, ordered a chicken calzone.

It was a god-awful chicken calzone.

A small woman in a raincoat and glasses bustled up and sat down next to me, clipping her umbrella closed with authority. She ordered a hot chocolate. Her hot chocolate arrived, an ode to sweet milky chocolate, so right for the weather. My calzone sat like a whale on my plate. The woman averted her eyes while she sipped steadily at her concoction.

She was the one who knew what to order, and I wanted to tell her so. I wanted to tell her how much I admired her choice of treat in the drizzle. And then to slide in a trite little comment about plant shops and pet stores side by side. Had she ever noticed? Had she ever in her life gone out strictly for flowers and cat food? And if so, did she know how easily that errand could be accomplished, just one block back?

UMBRELLAS

I know how to use an umbrella. I haven't lived in Southern California my entire life.

I lived in Florida once, for instance, for six years, and that is where I learned how to hoist an umbrella, learned to keep one with me at all times, and how to adjust for the direction of the rain.

In fact, my Florida umbrella was the one that went with me to Paris. I'd bought it in a drugstore, in a desperate moment, caught in an unexpected deluge. I paid ten dollars, and I planned to replace it as soon as I found myself in a place that sold fabulous umbrellas.

But I never did. Because this flimsy little umbrella did a superlative job. It turned out to be one tough little umbrella. So that when it came time to get a "decent" one for the boulevards of Paris, I couldn't. Such hardworking loyalty should be rewarded.

Rain. Love the thought of rain. Love the sound of rain. Was looking forward to rain in Paris. There's nothing more romantic than lamplight glowing on wet cobblestones, or the sound of raindrops on the roof lulling one to sleep. I understand I have the luxury of feeling this way because I live in SoCal, the land of white teeth and sunshine. And of course I totally appreciate clement weather. Of course I do.

However, I was looking for change. Weather is a convenient one. Northern Europe is dark and dreary. I lived in Brussels for three years. I'd been there—

But this was now. And I was looking forward to rain, okay?

Who knew October would be an absolutely gorgeous month in Paris. That the weather would be warm and sunny, just like spring. Maybe there's a hint of fall in the air, but not by much. Certainly not for the first three weeks of October.

Anyway, more than a little put out by these turns of events, I spent the first few weeks of the first trip trying to make my black upon black clothes lightweight enough to survive the ridiculous sunshine. People were actually wearing sandals, showing the state of their pedicures to the world. And seemed totally happy about it. I was peeling off layers of clothing all day.

I tried complaining about this miserable state of affairs to the few people I was beginning to meet. But the appalled looks I got shut me up immediately. I just had to suffer in silence. I did not find it in me to feel happy for sun-starved Parisians prancing blissfully around in their pastel summer clothes, napping in the sun on the green benches in the Luxembourg Gardens or the Champs de Mars, under the looming Eiffel Tower. Or those who tilted their faces reverently upward, soaking in some vitamin D directly from Mother Nature's primary source. Even the dogs were upwardly bound by the presence of the sunshine.

But one day I stepped out of my door, and oh my god, it was raining. Actually it was drizzling, but I didn't care.

I leapt back in the apartment and grabbed my trusty umbrella. I blew the dust off it, and hastened out to wallow in wet cobblestones and lamplight.

The Boulevard Sebastopol was bustling, crowded, all business. Hordes of people hastened up and down. This was not a tourist part of town. No one loitered or stood perusing their maps or took photos of every cranny they came across. There were no tourists from Newport Beach, California. And they were under no illusions that there was anything romantic about this particular burst of drizzle.

Not me. As far as I was concerned it was 1890 and I was in a Monet painting—

I unfurled my umbrella.

And before I could say *"Bonjour, M. Chevalier,"* I was thrown into the battlefield that is the Parisian sidewalk in the rain.

Suddenly umbrellas were coming at me from every direction. Suddenly I was going the wrong way on a high-speed highway. I panicked. Because I was going to crash into people. Eyes were going to be lost—

I was going to lose my umbrella, which used to be my friend, but now wasn't big enough, strong enough, or confident enough to survive this onslaught of professional rain people.

Hazards proliferated like the plague. I couldn't see where I was going. With the umbrella slanted at a forty-five-degree angle to keep the drizzle off my head, now all I could see were my chocolate suede boots. They were getting wet. I'd forgotten suede and rain are natural enemies. I'd forgotten that umbrellas are only good for keeping the top half of a person dry. I'd forgotten that the umbrella only keeps the head dry, and only if the tilt is just so.

There was no room and no time to keep the tilt just so.

Maybe the umbrella was going to be more trouble than it was worth.

Maybe it was confident people who had the strength of character who decided to hell with an umbrella. Like that thin man, striding along, thick scarf wrapped protectively around his neck, like it didn't matter the rest of his dapper outfit was getting wet. Or the woman with the dog who didn't seem to notice the rain at all.

I was getting shoved around out here on the Boulevard Sebastopol in the spattering rain—

Because it came down to this. It was war out there on the Boulevard Sebastopol in the rain. The battle was who would cave first and move their umbrella out of the way. Out of *my way* to be precise.

I should have had a marine with me. Better yet a tank.

I needed guidance. Maybe a three-week course on how to use an umbrella in the real world where people actually walk on sidewalks when it's raining.

I now realized I always had the place to myself in California when it rained, because Californians treat the arrival of rain like a typhoon has come to town. Schools close. No one goes out. The streets are deserted. It's the perfect day to make the hellish drive from Newport Beach to Santa Monica on the 405 because the freeways are empty.

Rain is glorified in Southern California. Rain is greeted with extreme enthusiasm. But one must stay home to both survive it and to take time to appreciate it. One spends much of a rainy day in SoCal staring at it pattering into the turquoise pool, while remembering those long ago days of childhood back on the East Coast, where rain was at one with the climate.

And in Florida, the only kind of rain is the torrential downpour, so that the dash from the car to the grocery store was the extent I actually had subjected myself to survival with my drugstore umbrella.

I knew now, bobbing and weaving with increasing ineffectiveness against the tides of humanity, buffeted from right to left, making no headway down the sidewalk whatsoever, that it had been but a delusion that I knew how to handle an umbrella in the rain. Eight million Parisians were on the attack. My version of good manners didn't stand a chance against the ruthless attack of French umbrella politesse.

So at first it was me who caved. I was the coward in the foreign land. I minced, bobbed, smiled apologetically, and all but threw my umbrella away, avoiding collision with one pushy Parisian pedestrian after the other. I was getting wet. I was losing the sense that all was well with my life. I was the underdog—

I'm no underdog.

Self-righteous indignation finally flared. I started holding my ground, which simply meant I stood still. This gave me a chance to see what was what.

It was young women who were running me down.

Oh yeah? Baby, I knew the type. I'd been that type. I remember how cool I was just because I was twenty-two. I remember how pitiless I was about the older person in my way.

But just because I remember being a jerk back then didn't mean I was going to do penance for it now. From my point of view, it was these young women who were going to show *me* some respect.

Seniority entitlement kicked in. I knew no fear.

It affected the stance of my umbrella. It affected the way

I held the tip of it to keep it from blowing away. It affected how I started to walk. As in straight into the oncoming umbrella traffic. This was no time for weakness. This was no time for half measures. I strode forward, prepared to actually collide—

So that now? I was emanating a new power, and the girls, still intensely aloof, did, at the very last moment, tip their umbrellas out of the way first.

Quel triomphe!

My status now improved, I was able to notice the rest of mankind out there. And that's when I noticed it was the elderly Parisian women who were suffused with an elegant graciousness their surly granddaughters ignored. They looked where they were going. They tipped their umbrellas out of the way, well in advance. They smiled slightly as we passed, acknowledging the folly of umbrellas in such a crowd. Sturdy on their feet, their umbrellas tipped graciously out of the way of my more unstable efforts, at ease with making their way for the likes of me, painfully new in town.

In the drizzle, calmer now, actually moving forward now, the hardworking Boulevard de Sebastopol took on the beauty of Monet. It was 1897, and the lamps were just being lit.

DAISY the GYPSY DOG

I met the dog one afternoon while sitting at the Café de Flores in St-Germain-des-Prés. I was in a total raging fit, trying to pull myself together.

The whole trip to Paris had gone completely sour because the construction being done on my building was god awful. Loud buzzing, sawing, and drilling, which started at 8:00 a.m., right outside my ground-floor windows. Which drove me from the apartment every morning like I was running from flames.

I'd ranted and raved about the situation finally to some new acquaintances, and by god, if one of them didn't say she might have an apartment for me—

So instead of flying back to California as in *right now*, I was toe tapping at the Café de Flores, waiting to hear if the other apartment was available.

Without asking, the dog joined me for lunch. She was a golden retriever, and she wore a kerchief around her neck. I named her instantly, in spite of myself. Daisy the Gypsy Dog.

I sat at a small table for one, outside, around the corner from the mob scene on the Blvd. St. Germain. I needed to be out of the teaming crowds. It had been two long weeks of brain-rattling noise at the apartment, with no kind of satisfaction coming from the rental company I used, and I would have killed them if I could have found them. I'd tried, but their office had moved. Hah!

However, I needed to pull myself together.

Next to me sat a handsome old man, dressed divinely, sipping a beer. There was a good-sized gold ring on his pinkie finger. He had a little book in front of him. It was a prop, because he never turned a page.

The waiter bustled up, pencil and order pad held in readiness. I asked for a menu. He froze. This happened every time with these waiters. What was with the simple request for a menu?

It wasn't until my second trip back to Paris that I realized that the very obvious menu written on the chalkboard by the front door of every café in Paris was there especially so I wouldn't need to ask for one, cutting by half the time it took to eat a meal alone in a café.

So, once more I thought, *Idiot* about the Parisian waiter when he looked put out by the request for a menu.

But he was young. I made myself smile. He was instantly mollified—

Maybe I reminded him of his mother?

He went for the menu.

Eventually I chose duck salad with a poached egg on it. I chose it for two reasons. The yolk would provide something runny.

The duck also screamed "daring." For an American woman of a certain age, I mean. Or so I told myself.

Anyway, the man next to me shifted approvingly when I said "Duck." He ordered an espresso. To sober up from the beer? Although he was too majestic and French to be done in by a single beer.

Daisy the Gypsy Dog showed up just as the duck did. She wandered casually up and down the bit of sidewalk where our tables were. She chose carefully. She chose me. Because—

I had the food. Of this, I was under no illusions.

The yellow retriever was intent on sharing my lunch with me. I know begging at the table is verboten among polite dog society...certainly in America. American dogs are a well-trained group. They've been to school. They go to play dates and dog parks to learn how to socialize. They have televisions in their cubbies when they are, god forbid, stashed away in a doggie hotel. And most definitely, they do not beg at the dinner table.

I can't say the dog begged exactly. She was a Parisian after all. But she gazed at me soulfully. I am a sucker for the soulful dog.

So, she gazed at me soulfully, then cast the barest flicker of an eye at my food.

"Non," I muttered politely but firmly, and was thrilled, I tell you, thrilled, when the dog dropped down by my feet, as if to say she understood about the food, but she hoped it would be okay with me if she just soaked in my presence, down here on the ground, by my feet.

The man's espresso was delivered. He shifted comfortably in his seat. I wanted to say something pithy, but I couldn't. I wanted to say something flirtatious, but I couldn't. I wanted to smile at him, but was afraid of being rude. Above all, I wanted to appear as though I knew what I was doing here at the Café des Flores.

So to that end I gave a whirl at eating my food the French way. That consisted of holding the fork down backwards on the plate, smashing the food onto the back of it with the knife, and bringing the fork up to my mouth upside down. Neither utensil is ever put down. One clutches them like bayonets.

Eating this way brought sweat to my brow, but I was doing a passable job. So, kudos to me, right? Eating duck and egg yolk, in the watery sunlight of a Paris corner, using my utensils like swords.

Except, suddenly Daisy was back on her feet. She almost but not quite lay her head on my knee. This time she openly stared at the duck and egg, followed by a swifter soulful look into my eyes. The man took a careful sip of his espresso.

I was a little firmer this time, myself.

"Non, ma chienne," I said. I petted her head. *"Non,"* I said, right into her flared nostrils.

Again she dropped to my feet. This time there was an audible sigh. Was she losing patience with me? Was I acting in a way that was worthy of losing patience with? After all, there was a mound of food on the plate.

The man took another sip of his espresso. I wanted to tell him to slow down, that his dollop of espresso would be long gone before I had the nerve to talk to him. Between the dog, the man, the duck—

The duck. Now the egg yolk was gone, and I had to make do with the very delicate amount of vinaigrette they'd dribbled on the meat and lettuce. Which meant I had totally lost interest. I hate dry food. I hate lettuce. I didn't like the duck, now that there wasn't any yolk left.

The dog sensed my agitation. She might be gaining here. Up she stood. Let me help you there, Madame, she seemed to say. Those big ole eyes looked at me full on.

I gazed back at her. There was total silence. The man's cup of espresso stopped midway to his mouth, his pinkie ring glinting in the light. The dog's eyes were deep and wise.

Give in, she was saying. You know you want to. You know you do. You were made to spoil beautiful animals like me. And I might even be starving. This might be my only meal this week. You don't know that for sure, now do you?

She never said please, though. Her tail was politely still. The French dog was simply feeling entitled. But why not? She knew without the egg yolk, there was no reason in the world to keep on eating the duck.

God, I hate duck.

But I love you, Dog, even though I know you are playing me like a violin.

I cut a piece of the duck. Sheepishly I glanced at the espresso drinker next to me. He beamed.

Aah. Okay. He approved.

I gave Daisy a piece of duck. She took it gently. She ate it expertly. She begged for the next piece. Expertly.

The man now ordered a cognac.

And there in the sun of St-Germain-des-Prés, I fed Daisy the rest of my lunch.

When I got up to leave, the man said, "Why don't you take her home?" He was so handsome. And I was tongue-tied.

"I'd love to," I said, "but I live in America."

"Ah yes. Where?"

"Los Angeles—"

"*Bon, bon.* The dog would love Los Angeles, I am sure."

"I want to live here and keep her here," I said.

"An even better idea," he said.

In the movie Ingrid Bergman would sit back down and one thing would lead to another—

But I was not Ingrid Bergman.

"Maybe someday soon—"

Hardly enough to have him leap up and offer me his entire carriage and fortune.

As for Daisy, I'm sure she went home that night to her Fagin. The kerchief spoke of loving hands somewhere. And she got to brag about the duck salad.

THE SHORT-ATTENTION-SPAN TOURIST

Immediately I started worrying about doing enough sightseeing—

Other people pretend they love sightseeing. That sightseeing is the raison d'être they travel.

I can't agree. I think sightseeing is overrated, and takes up too much time.

Furthermore, sightseeing can be tedious. It is a conduit for guilt—there are always more things to do and see than can be fit in. As a result, sightseeing is stress inducing and cliché ridden.

But since sightseeing came with the territory of a trip abroad, I had to make concessions. Even I had to admit that having come all the way to Paris there were some famous sights I should see. I did want to stand underneath the Eiffel Tower. I wanted to go to the Notre Dame, Ste. Chapelle, the Garnier, the Luxembourg Gardens, the Marais, the Jardin du Palais Royal in the neighborhood where Colette wrote. I couldn't be forced into the Louvre, but I was anxious to get to the Rodin. I looked forward to the boat trips on the Seine and the canal St. Martin. I knew I must have chocolate at Angelina's, and I wanted to check out every English bookstore in town, especially Shakespeare and Company bookstore.

But I would only do it in a seemly and efficient manner—

Which meant using a certain fastidiousness (being able to say no despite popular culture's opinion) in the choice-making process, and once underway, the sightseeing jaunt must be quick and to the point. Because by this stage of the game, I knew my short attention span had impacted nicely on my tolerance for sightseeing, so that I could let it flow. If I got bored in the Picasso Museum in two seconds flat, well then, I could leave. How much longer than ten minutes could I safely crane my neck staring up at the Eiffel Tower? And was it really necessary to stand in front of the Arc de Triomphe for any serious amount of time, after having had it in eyesight the whole way up the Champs-Elysées?

I wanted to let my sightseeing be so organic to the process of experiencing the place that I barely took photographs. I wanted to dissolve into the new atmosphere, picking and choosing my various destinations almost on the spur of the moment. And when needed I could skip my to-do list of sights for walks that went nowhere, much sitting in parks and riding metros and buses with nothing more in mind than the ride itself, and the taking of naps, even, yes, in the middle of sightseeing time.

In other words I planned to establish boundaries when it came to guilt sightseeing.

Which I did.

LAUNDRY

Ignoring the fact I was in Paris and therefore exempt from reality, laundry day arrived.

I am afraid of new appliances. My brief jet-lagged moment of defiance had worn off, and now I was really sorry I hadn't paid attention to Jacques.

Especially because the laundry contraption I faced was so teeth-churning chic, I knew I was in trouble.

It was a washer/dryer combination, supposedly washing and drying all in the same barrel. There had obviously been a contest for third-year design students, with the prize being immediate employment after graduation. Hence the result, now placed like a trophy, in a small cupboard in the small bedroom of my fabulously chic, but very small apartment.

I tiptoed over to it. My American lip curled. Two in one? Gimme a break. It'd never work. It was too sharp and minimalist to know anything about good old-fashioned washing and drying. And it was French, certain to be obtuse.

There was going to be trouble—

I like my clothes clean. I do my laundry often. *Merde, merde, merde.*

Cautiously I leaned in for a look at the dials. There were adorable little pictures on the dials. Intended to be clear as ice, I'm sure. Universal pictures. But for whom? I'm visual. I like visual. I can look at the clouds and find the dawn of creation in them. But pictures instead of words functioning as how-to, on a newfangled washer/dryer contraption? The pictures may as well have been in Chinese.

Then I looked closer, and, thank god, a few words emerged from the haze. French words. Strange-looking French words, although okay, I'd never done my laundry before in French. I grabbed my English/French dictionary…apparently the dictionary was not up on the latest laundry words either.

I paused, looking at the thing. There it sat, stuck in a back closet, a broom leaning on it, a vacuum cleaner tucked into the corner behind it, looking calm and Gallic.

"Just Do It" came to mind. But I'm not the sort who throws myself at a new mechanical object. I don't flip switches, press buttons, twirl dials, or otherwise launch into the unknown, figuring, *How hard can it be?* I don't have a single natural instinct for mechanical things.

The machine sat there, unforgiving and precise.

I knew defeat. I put laundry day on hold, called Jacques, and made an appointment for Saturday.

Saturday and Jacques arrived. This time I took notes. And when he left I gave it a shot.

Jacques' instructions called for using the "sun dry" option of the drying process. Which was, I guess, the kind of drying that was kind to clothes. Jacques had assured me that my clothes would be washed in the time-honored tradition. Then, sitting inside the same bin in which they had been washed, "sun dry" would commence, and after a while my clothes would be dry.

How this was to succeed, I couldn't even begin to fathom.

The wash cycle started. This cycle sounded as it should. There was running water and all—

The washing cycle went on a long time. I read something soothing, sitting on the couch. I tried to ignore the fact that it was Saturday afternoon in Paris, and I was inside doing laundry. I was even suffering anxiety over the process, which upset me because I hadn't expected anxiety from this particular source.

The washer cycle did end, finally.

The "sun dry" portion started. That is, I heard one button click off, and another button click on. I tiptoed over, and sure enough, "sun dry" was now illuminated. I waited for sounds of tumbling—

Silence.

I opened the top so I could see the tumbling, drying clothes come to a halt. I was prepared to offer homage to the third-year law student for my pointless doubt. I was looking forward to being amazed at just how silent the sound of drying clothes could be.

There was no tumbling. The clothes were sitting in a wet jumble. Near as I could tell there was no hot air either. There seemed to be a warm haze to it all, though. Maybe the warm haze would get warmer. I closed the lid, and went back to my seat on the couch. I commenced to doze.

After fifty-five minutes of total silence from the washer/dryer, during which hot air, or maybe not so hot air, supposedly wafted around my wet clothes, a binger went off. The binger sounded completely sure of itself.

I opened the lid. Frankly I was expecting damp clothes. And that is exactly what I got.

On the dials and buttons there was no obvious way to add fifteen more minutes of this. I was going to a book reading at the Red Wheelbarrow, so, not allowing myself to swear or do any other psychologically damaging behavior, I scattered the dampish clothes all over the apartment and left, my hair standing on end.

A few days later I attempted another load. After fifty-five minutes of the "sun dry" thing, I bravely asked the machine for more time…fifteen measly minutes. At least, that's what I hoped I asked for. Just fifteen minutes more of wafting warmish air through my clothes all sitting in a heap at the bottom of the well.

Was this too much to ask?

The washer/dryer shut off.

Merde.

So, next load I took a bigger chance. Saying a small prayer, I asked for "tumble dry," even though Jacques had (pointedly?) ignored explaining the tumble dry option.

The contraption took umbrage—

I got no dry at all.

I took umbrage. Snarling, I ran the fool washer through again. I banged in "sun dry" and didn't bother to pray. But now the washer/dryer was angrier than me, and wouldn't give me "sun dry" either. So that now my clothes had been washed through twice, soaked through twice, without even a "sun dry" to call their own.

Soaking wet clothes now hung all over the apartment.

But I rallied. I was in Paris, right? I became creative. I loaded up panties, socks, bras, t-shirts on the wooden hangers, and color coordinated each one with the furniture or banister upon which they were hanging. I managed to thank the French for that successful contraption, the towel rack heater. What hung there got seared dry, pronto. So then it was just a matter of rotating the laundry.

It took three days to complete this load of wash.

Thereafter I approached the machine bowing and scraping, asking only for "sun dry." Now a permanent part of the décor was dampish clothes fluttering about everywhere. Like flags. Like banners. Often startling me as I rounded a corner or caught a flutter out of the corner of my eye.

Charmingly bohemian, I muttered to myself, eating three chocolate croissants in a row to ease the pain.

"It takes forever to dry your clothes in France."

This should be printed in bold at the top of your precious airline ticket.

FATHER AND SON

The Champs de Mars is beautiful park that stretches out in front of the Eiffel Tower. Majestic Belle Epoque edifices lining either side of this wide expanse which transport me right back to my life in Brussels—

Every day my school bus had stopped in front of apartments just like these, and Johnson Delaney and his sister got on. Johnson was in my class. He had beautiful gray eyes. The irises were outlined in black, and rimmed by mink-like eyelashes. The beauty of his eyes was further magnified by Johnson's thick glasses. He was obviously a bookish and gentle soul, even at twelve years old. I was madly in love, on all of those bus rides, but even then, without knowing what I knew, I knew his heart was not into girls.

But so, I was walking here one day, one foot back in Brussels. The path through the Champs de Mars is wide here. Almost a road, not paved. Gold dirt, and well padded. Suitable for strollers like myself. There were also joggers. This was jarring to me as joggers seem so…American. Parisians don't seem the sort to jog, as it is a most ungainly pursuit when you think about it. Particularly for the socially self-conscious Parisian—

But wait…stereotyping is so wrong, right?

Anyway, I was walking toward the Eiffel Tower when I beheld, in the distance, a large man pounding down the red dirt road toward me. Beside him was a smallish object. At first I thought it was his dog. Now this was definitely not Parisian—man jogging with dog? A Parisian *dog* would not be caught dead jogging, for god's sake.

Let alone a man…with dog, I mean.

So I stared. This I had to see. What kind of Parisian man would be caught out running with his dog?

I fished my sunglasses out of my sac so I could stare more discreetly.

Gradually the object running alongside the man morphed into a small bicycle. Still committed to my dog-at-his-side fantasy, now it seemed to me the man was actually out running with his bicycle. Since it certainly wasn't a pet, maybe it was a posh new addition to jogging gadgets, such as a gait measurer?

But of course it couldn't be.

Setting a brisk pace, man and his bicycle approached rapidly. I slowed my pace. And finally what I was looking at slid into focus.

It was a small boy pedaling on a bicycle. Father and son, I immediately assumed. The little boy, who looked very little at this distance, was pedaling ferociously. Pedaling his little rear off to keep up with the old man…French though they might both be, and above that kind of public display of exertion.

They got closer, and I saw that the father was Scottish looking. He was tall with a stocky build, had red hair, a beard, and was wearing regular jogging fare—shorts, tank top, well-used running shoes, and most of all, the sweatband. The sweatband always gives the jogger that look of authority. If they are sporting a baseball cap, one can rest assured they are but neophytes, and about to keel over.

This fine specimen of a man was steaming along. And next to him Junior. Let me call him Philippe. Philippe also had the red hair, but at his age, which looked about six years old, it was still a mass of red-orange curls springing out all over his head. This hair, while a joy to his maman, could only have been a source of despair for Philippe.

But so, he had that hair. And as they got closer (and I had all but stopped) I could see he was clad in slacks, a shirt, and a long-sleeved, v-necked, Argyle sweater. His shoes were Oxfords. Tied. Not a slap of Velcro to be seen. I couldn't see the crease in his little trousers, but I was sure there was one. I was also immediately sure he had chosen his own outfit this morning, without any help from anyone, thank you very much.

Given his meticulous street clothes and Papa's jogging gear, I immediately detected a trace of personality differences, shall we say, and it seemed that Philippe had been dragged straight from school by Papa here. It appeared that Papa had scheduled one hour this week to be with his son, and figured to do it right by getting the little bookworm away from the books into the fresh air, running and laughing with his Papa. Having, in general, a very manly and athletic hour.

After all, it is quality not quantity that matters, especially if you are as important as Papa most definitely was.

As the duo approached, a huge wave of pity for Philippe welled up within my snooping soul. I thought I should send the little guy a huge wave of karmic sympathy as they passed by. Maybe it would help—

And then they sailed by. And I saw that—

Petit Philippe was Rambo. He most definitely did not

need my sympathy. He roared by, pedaling furiously, cheeks red with determination, his face set in stone. He was in no way intimidated by his big Papa here, who'd probably shown up at school to drag him out of his chess tournament (which he was winning) for this incredible moment of father/son bonding…running and biking in the wind on the Champs de Mars. If that was what the old man wanted, then Junior here was more than happy to oblige, and not even break a sweat, because there was no way in hell he was going to mess up his clothes, or forget the feel of his knight he had been about to move, so that later tonight, he could tell Maman and Grand Mere what move he'd been about to make, before being so rudely interrupted.

And what Papa didn't know was that he was also training on the sly to surprise the old man (because he did love his *cher* Papa, despite obvious personality differences) by demanding he be allowed to go on the next mountain-climbing spree.

Maman would throw a fit, but Papa was a French father after all—

Philippe, making his Papa proud beyond words, would be allowed to climb the mountain, which he'd enjoy a whole lot more than this stupid moment of pedaling like a maniac on this stupid little bike, forgoing the chess match, just to reassure his *cher* Papa that he knew how to be a man.

PANIC at L'OPERA GARNIER

I made the mistake of letting my friend Natalie buy our tickets to the ballet at the Opera Garnier. And found out too late that she believed to the bottom of her heart the only way to experience ballet was by hanging around up in the rafters.

I arrived early. Still jet-lagged, on this my second trip. Still whirling in disbelief that I was back in Paris after a year. But acclimated enough to know how to negotiate the harrowing walk from the metro, while trying to steal peeks at the beautiful, gilded Opera Garnier, home of Paris National Ballet Company.

Crossing the boulevard there is more fearsome than normal, because L'Opera metro station is placed right in the center of Place de L'Opera. So that it is surrounded by twenty thousand lanes of blaring, chaotic traffic whirling around the island metro station like crazed whales. Emerging up from the bowels of Paris to find myself in the midst of such cacophony and rushing bodies, and frayed nerves…well, it swept me off my feet most unpleasantly the first time there. But this time, even wearing delicate go-to-the-ballet clothes, I knew that getting across the boulevard would be doable—

Because I tailgated those who were in the know. I chose those whose noses were held confidently aloft, as they marched out into the mayhem of cars, busses, motorcycles, and Smart cars. I practically held onto their coattails. If I got a look for being too close, I just swept an indignant glance at the space behind me, as though I too were being harassed by scaredy cats stepping on my heels. Damn tourists.

It was like stepping out into a stampeding herd. Especially as the particularly long crosswalk leading straight to the sweeping steps of the Garnier did not have traffic lights.

I chose a Coco Chanel reincarnate and her much younger companion. They had the air of absolute rightness of being. I huddled in. They moved forward. I took a breath and followed. Cars stopped. There was no screeching. No surprises for the Paris driver here at the Garnier, apparently. They stopped to let the crowds of ballet goers reach their destination intact.

Suddenly I was on the steps of the Garnier, soaking in the magnificent people watching. And such people watching! It turned out to be people watching at its highest level and should be listed in tourist guides.

There were black on black ensembles to die for. Much velvet. Many hats. Black stockings. Men in cashmere scarves. Berets too. There was a huge amount of noxious but sexy smoking going on, with that graceful swooping of the hand, the flurry of chatter accompanied by a halo of smoke. There were joyful greetings, and carefully suave, low-keyed greetings. There were large groups, entwined duos, elderly elegance, more smoking, and of course some pouting.

I was wearing brown, but it worked. I had on a light tweed pinstriped pants suit, tailored within an inch of its life, with a slight flair of the jacket at the waist. Cuffs on the trousers. My scarf was white and dripping with beads, embroidery, and fringe. Very 1920s, see. In LA my outfit would have seemed pointlessly daytime Katharine Hepburn. Until maybe they noticed the blue suede three-inch heels I could barely walk in, and would never, ever wear again. But here in Paris, every inch of it worked.

Thank god. Because I fret over such details.

Natalie finally arrived. Beyond late. I had gone from having a divine time people watching, to controlled rage that she was late, again, and would arrive as if nothing was wrong.

But since I hadn't seen her in a year, when she did finally glide up to me, effortlessly Parisian chic meets Yankee forbearers, well, what the heck.

Until it turned out that—

Our seats were at the zenith of the opera house.

We rushed in, having barely bussed each other's cheek. There was no time to linger in the opulent Second Empire interior. The marble, the amber light from the gilded candelabras lining the sweeping curved staircases, the rugs, the chandeliers dripping with crystal, all passed by in a blur as we tore up five thousand flights of stairs. Apparently this was quicker than the elevator, for which I was half grateful, because I loathe and fear elevators, especially Parisian ones.

We ran up and up. I didn't keep track of how high. I just kept wondering when Natalie would keel over, which took my mind off my own miserable state. My three-inch heels were wrong, oh so wrong, for this.

I was staggering, on the verge of a heart attack when we finally climbed the last little flight of steps to the right door. Natalie handed the tickets to the usher, who gestured where we should go, and we burst out at the very top of the opera house, the stage but a dot ten thousand feet below.

It was too late to scream.

Natalie sailed forth and immediately disappeared from my view as she leapt lightly down the stairs to the very front of this very highest balcony seating. In white fear, unable to breathe, barely able to suppress the urge to drop to my knees and crawl, I teetered down the many steps from the top of the balcony to the very front row of it. Black spots in front of my eyes, a high hum in my ears, I followed Natalie as we crawled over several venerable old women. Natalie, practiced and sure, listed away from the endless drop. I desperately emulated her. Finally we sat down in seats that were the size of first-grade desks. The space was so narrow my knees pressed against the ledge of the balcony, which had absolutely no guardrail. So there I sat, in the front row of the highest balcony in the place, a chasm below me, making death by falling a definite possibility.

Natalie happily bustled about getting comfortable in her seat. I wanted to kill her. But I couldn't move, although every bone in my body screamed for flight. I was too petrified to move. I was convinced if I moved so much as an inch, vertigo would hurl me over the edge, and not even the thought of the proper Parisians on whose laps I would land soothed my panic.

This was no state in which to enjoy the gilded surroundings. If I hadn't been frozen in terror, I would have killed my dear friend Natalie, who continued chattering most charmingly about this and that, including the noisy woman who came in after us, acting as though she were on the ground floor. I hated her for her calm. How long had it taken these apparently sane people to adjust to this godforsaken height, this incredibly dangerous place? No guardrail? What this something chicly European, or rather an arrogant oversight?

Actually, with no experience whatsoever of sitting in

rafter seats, I had no idea if life was as dangerous as this in all the opera houses of the world.

But I was in a full-blown panic attack, with nowhere to run. I couldn't take it. I was gonna die. Die right here, up in the stratosphere. Don't think. That's what I thought. Shut up! I had a few tricks, for godsake. So use them—

I prayed. To God, Buddha, and whomever might be listening. I kept my eyes staring straight ahead, which meant I had full view of the huge chandelier, a perfect view of Chagall's masterful ceiling. Photo op supreme. So, never letting my eyes veer downward, and thinking this might take my mind off where exactly I was, I felt for my purse, lifted it to my lap without breathing, and found my camera. I commenced to point blindly and snap.

The ballet started. Camera was carefully put away. I tried to cut deals with myself to ignore the GREAT FALL. I wanted to see the ballet, goddammit. I continued to lean back as far as I could without falling into the knees of the person sitting behind me. I tried to look down—

The floor tilted.

But after a long while, well into the ballet, my heart did slow down. If I cared to note, I said to self, it did appear as though I wasn't going to fall over the edge. And frankly, I said to myself, oh so earnestly, hands in prayer position, if there was any real danger way up here, the area wouldn't be open to the public, would it?

Gradually panic faded away. Gradually what I was seeing came into focus. And gradually, while never relaxing completely, I became enthralled in the performance.

It was *Wuthering Heights*, which turns out to be a potboiler of a story. This staging translated into a lot of languorous, sensual, and sexually ambiguous pas de deux, with all sorts of characters falling in love and having ballet sex, and raging at each other right afterward, and falling, therefore, out of love, and crying and dying and so on.

While coming to terms with the fact that I didn't know what the hell was really going on, I also finally noticed that the sets, which were odes to Zen simplicity, countered nicely with the bodice-ripping story.

From here one had a perfect view of the stage floor. Not a pretty sight. It was filthy. My teeth were on edge as to whether or not the gauzy, pastel costumes would survive the dust and the dirt.

But from these seats, now that I could shift my eyes oh so carefully downward, I saw that I had a perfect view of the orchestra in their pit. This was indeed a sublime view of the orchestra—

Which almost made up for the seats.

By the end I could breathe. My armpits had dried. And I could speak to Natalie without screaming.

I did, however, make it quite clear that I could never, ever sit up that high ever again.

So, to this day, when we go to the theatre together, she gets my seat way down in the middle of orchestra, and she sits up there with the angels, and when we meet in the middle at intermission, we talk about everything but this divergence of opinion.

THE EIFFEL TOWER
AND ME

I could have sworn the Eiffel Tower was red back in 1962, the first time I saw it. Okay, maybe rust. But definitely not the gray it is now.

But I can find no reference to the Eiffel Tower ever being red. No matter how many times or how many different ways I Google "red Eiffel Tower."

I've had to let that notion go. It's difficult.

Back then I, of course, thought it was stupid. I was twelve. I was cosmopolitan, okay? If my parents were going to drag me away from the United States, where I could have been a cheerleader, to Brussels, Belgium, where cheerleading wasn't even on the agenda at the International School of Brussels (oh there are pictures in my yearbooks of some older girls pretending what they are doing is cheerleading, but let me tell you, it wasn't the same thing at all), then just too sophisticated for words would be what I would become.

So of course I didn't thrill to the Eiffel Tower. It looked ridiculous. And no, I would not climb up to wherever, with my little brother. I'd already made that mistake in Rome at

St. Peter's, thank you very much. So my little brother set off by himself in a huff, and I rode the elevator to the first level, got off, and waited. Lounging by the top of the stairs, older sister know-it-all dripping from my red coat. And sure enough, by the time my brother reached me, he was white and gasping, and ready to go home to America too. I led him gently to the elevator, into which he got without a peep for the return trip down.

Now, of course, I love the Eiffel Tower. It is a beautiful thing. Massive and tall. Lacy and graceful. It really can be seen from just about anywhere. It's one of the wonders of the world. Not just because of its appearance, but because it is so loved.

I loved to stroll in the Champs de Mars. I loved to hang out underneath it. I loved to sit in the great park, staring up at it. The Eiffel Tower was elegant. It was grand. It was beautiful, in all its filigreed splendor.

And I especially loved to watch people from all over the world come and stare happily and hungrily up at it. It's an affirmation for living in peace. One time I was hastening home through the Champs de Mars, and I passed a young German couple running happily toward it. They were holding hands and gazing upward, both dazzled. Awe showing in their faces—

And right behind them, going more slowly, was an elderly Asian couple. Also holding hands. Also gazing upward reverentially.

Right underneath it were carnival-like food stands. Also many selling trinkets. There were now roped areas in which to stand in line waiting to ascend. Zillions of people were milling about, but the Eiffel Tower was so huge that standing underneath it was like being in a vast train station.

One windblown day I was there, on my way to somewhere else. As an adult who was not a mere tourist, but also somewhat a resident, by virtue of the fact I had to go to the grocery store regularly, I mainly got my Eiffel Tower fill on the sly. From the bridges crossing the Seine. Standing over in the Tuileries. Or simply rushing home from the American Library.

Anyway, this day it was cold. And I was starving. For the first time I actually registered the food stands. One in particular seemed to be bellowing out more smoke than the rest. And the line was longer than the others.

I drifted closer and sniffed the luscious smell of frying grease. I make no apologies. For some it's chocolate for breakfast. For me, it's grease all the way.

I inhaled deeply. And then, omigod, an odor straight from my years in Brussels hit my nostrils. It was *gaufres*…waffles…to be eaten with mounds of powdered sugar. Omigod. I began to salivate. Memories of going to the traveling carnivals and gorging on the sweet waffles right off the griddle warming us up on those dreary Belgian winter days burst forth. I stopped and paid overdue homage to the fact that living in Brussels had not been all bad, and most especially when it came to food, and most especially of all when it came to *gaufres*.

I wanted one immediately. I wanted two.

And then I thought, where there are *gaufres*, there are *pomme frites*.

Pomme frites were sold on the street corners in Brussels, wrapped up in a cone of newspaper, heavily salt and peppered and served with a large dollop of mayonnaise on top. Always too hot to eat at first. Oh, the wait until the fries were cooled down enough to handle. This unbelievable treat alleviated the chill as well. Assuaged an ill temper.

I sniffed some more. I stood swaying in the cool breeze of *gaufre* grease, and yes, now I smelled the *pommes frites*.

Omigod. I was starving. Memories were flying in. That particularly brilliant batch of frites at the harbor in Antwerp. God, it had been cold that day. Or those *gaufres* at the carnival in Tervuren, the suburb of Brussels where we actually lived, and where for once the lady sprinkled on too much powdered sugar—

I wanted *pommes frites* now. I wanted, no, craved *gaufres*, now. Mayonnaise. Powdered sugar. I wanted…I needed—

But the line was so long.

But hey, it was moving. A little delayed gratification might be a good thing—

I floated back in time, and got in line.

Every crumb was spectacular. Every morsel was as good as it had been when I was twelve.

RETURNING LE LISSEUR

I could have accessed my inner Frenchwoman, shrugged my shoulders, and let it go.

But no. It had become a matter of principle. Was I an American or a mouse?

The flat-iron issue had appeared when my own died the minute it set foot in France. God knows why. Had the flight been too damn long? Didn't like the transformer?

So I trudged over to the dreary Monoprix, heart heavy. The Monoprixs are France's version of Target. At home, I appreciate Target, but it's certainly no love affair. In Paris, I hated the Monoprix. I'd already had to go there for hangers and a spatula. Having failed to anticipate domestic errands into my Paris life formula, shopping for hangers and a spatula had not been a pretty experience.

So here I was, again. This time in search of a flat-iron. It took a bit. I had to hesitantly query several salespersons. But eventually one was found, paid for, and carried home.

The new flat-iron looked benign. But the instruction book was not. It took hours to decipher. It was written in twenty-seven languages, with a font so small as to be invisible, and was heavy as a box of large nails. The instructions were brief as well. As you can imagine. Whoever wrote the thing must have had a nervous breakdown after language number seventeen. I mean, how interesting can such a task be?

After a bout of serious reading, I plugged the new flat-iron in. Not only did the little green light, which I had been told was the sign to look for announcing it was successfully turned on, did not blaze forth, but there didn't seem to be the slightest amount of heat emitting from the prongs.

Hope refusing to be quashed, I read the instructions written in French, just in case I'd missed something in the English version. It seemed I had not. So then I began a series of hopeless maneuvers to get the sucker to light up, maybe a little heating up as well. I plugged it into every socket in the apartment.

But no. Absolutely no lighting up. Absolutely no heating up.

I stared in mute disbelief at the instruction manual written in twenty-seven languages. Seemed an irresponsible effort in light of the flat-iron's ensuing behavior.

I have to take it back, I thought. My heart sank. God no. Not the Monoprix… again.

But I'd paid good money for the flat-iron.

I wanted, no, needed, my euros back.

Three days later, basically terrified but grimly determined, I walked back to the Monoprix to return the unspeakable flat-iron.

I arrived as prepared as I could be. I'd looked up the word for "flat-iron" in my French/English dictionary. It was "lisseur."

I walked in the door and took a breath. *"Bonjour, Madame—"*

She immediately waved me to someone else.

It took several inquiries to begin the process. But finally

the young cashier on the second floor, after recoiling from the notion she simply refund me my money, managed to find two saleswomen willing to deal with the situation.

So there I stood, two unsmiling saleswomen looking at me, then raising their eyebrows at each other. Assessing my fortitude?

Well, I'd been in Paris for ten days. I knew what to do. I stared at the floor, the *lisseur*, the shoes of one of the saleswomen, which happened to be aging Nikes. I did not look into their eyes. I did not smile.

They stared at me and the flat-iron some more. The clucks of disapproval, though silent, filled the air. "Where's the plug," said one of them finally, after apparently being unable to convince even themselves that I would willfully return a functioning appliance.

I wanted to run—

But I wanted my euros more. I would consider it a win, a triumph, in fact. That was the bottom line. So far I hadn't won the few battles I'd chosen to fight. But this time, this time by God, I had truth and justice on my side.

What I didn't have on my side were these two steely-eyed French matrons who were in no hurry to render a decision.

"Where's the electrical outlet?"

A wash of panic suffused my American being. Could I trust the French *lisseur* to do the right thing and remain malfunctioning?

A socket was shown to her. She pulled the *lisseur* out of its French box. You better not work, Princess, I thought. But this was Paris. This was a French flat-iron. I couldn't count on it to do the right thing.

Saleslady number one pulled it out of its box. She fussed a moment with the entwined cord. She plugged it in.

The *lisseur* did not light up. The *lisseur* did not heat up. The *lisseur failed* to function.

Hot triumph lit every inch of my body. I wanted to grab it and kiss it. I could barely hold back a manic grin.

There was a deep silence, which was a difficult moment. I knew I must remain silent. I had a husband who once told me all good salesmen know that once a sale is made, shut up—

A formidable concept.

Because now I wanted to burst forth with a kind of sheepish goodwill, hoping to spare them the possible embarrassment of having sold me a defective *lisseur* in the first place. I wanted to babble on how my own flat-iron died on me the instant I attached it to the transformer I'd brought with me. I wanted to tell them I was in Paris for six weeks all by myself, and wasn't that totally fantastic, and indeed everything was fantastic until this very defective *lisseur* entered my life, and unfortunately, as a result I had been forced to return it to the Monoprix, ruining, thereby, their day.

But I didn't. I kept my mouth shut. I stole another happy peek at the still non-functioning *lisseur*. The heat of triumph had another moment.

Triumph made me confident, which was a hell of a lot better than diffident. Has being diffident ever done anyone any good? Especially here in Paris, in front of two hefty saleswomen?

Yes, confidence swept in, and I could practically taste the sixty euros I was about to get back. I was even prepared for what most likely would be the next question. And sure enough it came.

"Would Madame like another *lisseur*?"

Madame would not like another *lisseur*. Madame wanted her money back.

I pursed my lips like I'd seen everyone do. I took a moment to appear to think about the possibility that I might want another of their flat-irons.

I paused, choosing my severely limited words with care.

"No," I said in French. I paused again. "No thank you, Mesdames, but no. No, I do not want another *lisseur*."

"Please then, your credit card."

Yeah, right—

"I paid with euros," I said.

I hazarded a glance at them now. They hung over the sales receipt in total disbelief. It seemed this money was going to come out of the mouths of their children.

However, they were Parisians. Butter wouldn't...you know. By some unseen dose of steel, they regained their composure. The *lisseur* was shoved back into its box. They turned to the young salesclerk manning the cash register, and with an eloquent nod, silently instructed her to issue me my cash.

I caught the pupils of her eyes widen for just a second. Then never glancing at me again, she unglued the euros from the register, and handed them to me.

I floated to the metro.

OPINIONS
IN THE PARC MONCEAU

The Parc Monceau is considered *tres chic*. It has an illustrious history of design. I wanted to love it. In fact I was prepared to positively adore it. It sounded mouth watering.

But it turned out to be a little piece of America. I was *tres* disappointed. Yes, there were follies and plant-covered colonnades, carefully situated ponds, mini waterfalls described so adoringly in the travel guide, but I saw a grand park straight out of Disneyland or the Boston Commons. The guidebook praised this park for its naturalness, which it claimed was a nice difference from the formality of the Luxembourg Gardens, the Place des Vosges, or the gardens of the Palais Royal—

Whatever. I was not looking for the San Diego Zoo that day. I'd been promised Belle Epoque. Certainly the environs over there in the eighth screamed enough Belle Epoque for me, who will never tire of that era. But in Parc Monceau itself?

It had taken three metros to get there, at a time I was still emerging in triumph whenever I got to my destination just as planned. So I stayed. Nose flaring, I stayed, but I was going to try to be open. Nothing wrong with American parks.

It was Saturday morning. There were joggers, for start-ers. Pounding along the paths with fierce determination. I hadn't seen joggers in quantity in Paris so far. And these joggers were type A sorts, in their thirties, wearing deluxe running clothes, and god forbid, I even saw baseball hats. Maybe these were American expat joggers?

But in fact these weren't even joggers. These were runners. Runners run hard. They wear watches and iPods while running. They do not wear ratty t-shirts and beat-up running shorts, like mere joggers do. Runners shake the earth as they sprint by, all ferocious and focused. They make noise as they steam by. They intrude on one's person-al Saturday morning calm (in spite of having found oneself in a little bit of St. Louis right here in gay Paree). They are best avoided.

Bravely ignoring the heavy breathing, I strolled on.

There was a lot going on in the Parc Monceau that Saturday morning.

I leaned over the railing of a Hansel and Gretel bridge and saw ducks paddling in a pretty alpine-like streamlet, and while I thought it was pretty and all, I also thought about how ducks in metropolitan areas can be one step away from being an all-out nuisance.

I didn't know this until I lived in Jacksonville, Florida, for six years. While there I learned that it is a bad thing if you look out your back door one morning and see a mother duck and her babies floating so adorably in your swimming pool. What will follow is an invasion of vermin-ridden ducks. Your children will be enthralled, but you will have to keep your children out of the now infested pool, until one day they come home from school and find no more ducks and a drained swimming pool.

If you are a smart parent you will deny any knowledge of what possibly could have happened—

Unless your children are ten and over. Then you will have to tell them the truth, and be prepared to be called a murderer. They may even wake up with nightmares and disrupt your sleep for days on end.

Or you can avert the whole disaster by buying a house with the pool already covered by a huge dome of mesh, even though it will be an eyesore that will annoy you the whole time you live in Florida.

Or you could come to Paris to find perhaps the beginning of the exact same problem.

Parc Monceau had confection stands. So did the Champs de Mars. So did the Luxembourg Gardens. The Tuileries too.

But they did not sell cotton candy, like the Parc Monceau did. Cotton candy belongs in America, at county fairs where one also stares at pet goats and pigs as big as houses.

Besides, cotton candy creates the crying child because the thing is ungainly and easily dropped.

And it was true, there were crying children in the Parc Monceau that morning, standing howling with a cone of pink spun sugar lying in the dust by their shoes.

Is it possible to picture cotton-candy-eating French children? Enough to induce schizophrenia.

But, just in time to bring a little French to the outing, I noticed the statues. These statues are much touted statues of great writers in their finest Belle Epoque haughtiness, each with a swooning muse draped around their feet.

I wondered about this. Actually I had a fit about it. Statues proudly displayed of old men with young women hanging onto their feet?

Maybe the sculptor who had received the original commission just hated doing feet. Had issues with sculpting feet. Feet were too hard to do—

So that is why he'd draped the muses thusly.

Another way he avoided doing the feet was by putting Ambroise Thomas, for example, in a dressing gown. So that it was amidst the swirls of his robe at the bottom of his legs that his muse gazed up at him with committed adoration.

The dressing gown could have also been because the sensibilities of the sculptor were such that he couldn't put his muses down at the end of a pair of trousers, because those trousers would have been dragged in the dirt, this being the days of horse-drawn carriages, which means the roads were chock full of piles of dung—

It just wouldn't have done to have a delicate, swooning muse getting dung all over her pale fingers and even lips as she kissed so passionately, clinging so tightly to those soiled trousers, no matter how committed her adoration.

The statues got my goat. I sat down on a green bench to brood, this being a sunny Saturday morning, filled with the sounds of falling cotton candy and thudding running shoes.

Why weren't there statues of women writers with their male muses swooning? Was this because women don't like their muses to swoon? Or is it because male muses don't swoon, and in fact men aren't looking for the muse job?

I know George Sand loved her tubercular Chopin, and she did seem the sort who would have been tickled by a little swooning. But, frail and wispy though he was, Chopin didn't need to swoon. He was a world-famous composer.

Sand and Chopin were out and about in Paris during the time these statues were made. It wouldn't have been out of context to include Sand (a great writer) and Chopin. George certainly would have been ready to dress up in her male clothes. She would have been just fine, in fact, on a rearing horse, and probably would have picked the pose if only they'd asked.

But Chopin...he desisted. Even a frail composer, pretty much dying of tuberculosis his whole life, would never have consented to gazing up at Sand from her feet.

Which is where I think women finally are today.

CHRISTOFFE

In California, I went to my hairdresser before I left. "Will my color last till I get back?" You'd think he'd lie—

"No," he said.

"Damn," I said.

I was also growing my hair out.

So in this state of dishabille, I was going off to Paris, France, where I would have to find a hair salon (which I didn't think would prove difficult). Then I would have to choose one (which I did). And finally, most daunting of all, I would have to enter the chosen salon and throw myself on the mercy of impossibly bored twenty-four-year-olds. I would need to gain their respect in broken French. And I would need to convince them I wasn't kidding about my hair color. Marilyn Monroe, not Grace Kelly.

Merde.

I actually considered forgoing the entire trip, but sanity won out. I boarded the jet. I'd worry about it later.

By the time it became necessary to deal with my hair, I was an old hand at Paris, see, and a little more relaxed and a little more French-like in my ways. More importantly, I now had my friend Natalie, and she, naturally, had a hairdresser.

"I love him," she said with a conviction I found immediately comforting.

His name was Christoffe.

"Will you come with me to translate?" I asked. All but prostrating myself at her feet.

"No," she said.

"Will you at least make the appointment?"

She'd raised three children. "No."

She did deign to give me his number. Thank god, because the Parisian telephone book was laid out backward, and apparently written in Hindi.

The time came to make the call. I sat on the edge of the bed sucking deep, quieting breaths. It was hard enough understanding the French when I could actually see their faces and read their lips, but over the phone, those visual aids were gone. The few phone calls I'd made hitherto, those to French-speaking people, as opposed to Natalie, or the director of the American Library, hadn't gone well. Basically, I'd panic, and hang up.

But my hair had to be dealt with. End of story.

So I closed my eyes, the better to concentrate both on his French and mine, and dialed.

The dial tone in Paris is like a bleating foghorn. Doesn't sound like the phone is ringing at all. Sounds like there's a problem. But I held tight. I now knew the phone was indeed ringing—

A man answered. I think he said he was Christoffe.

"Christoffe?" I asked anyway. Making sure my "r" at least was just right.

"Oui, Madame."

"I am an American. My friend is Natalie, and she gave me your number."

"Oui, Madame?"

"Do you know Natalie?" I needed to make sure he knew Natalie. Because if not, I could hang up right then.

"Oui, Madame."

"Okay…ummm, I speak very little French—"

"Ah no, Madame, you speak very well."

"Merci," I trilled, in spite of myself. "I need to make an appointment for my hair," I said.

"For your hair. Yes, Madame." Was that a smile in his voice?

"Umm yes, my hair. I need color and a little trim." I'd even looked up "trim" in my French/English dictionary. In fact I was super prepared for this call—

And I was wondering why I made such heavy weather of making business calls back home. I was thinking, god, the calls are in *English*. How simple can it be?

Christoffe was saying something. It ended with a question mark. All I heard was the silence after the question mark.

"What?" I said, niceties falling by the wayside. Including the use of the word "Monsieur," which would have been appropriate. *"Pardon, Monsieur?"* I should have said. And actually I shouldn't even have had to ask. I should have been paying attention, and not wandering off into the issue I have with making phone calls at home.

Christoffe finished repeating himself.

Merde. "Pardon, Monsieur. What did you say?" I tried to put a smile into the question.

Christoffe apparently had the patience of Job. "When would you like to come in, Madame?"

When? Besides never?

"Er, Monday or Tuesday is good for me." Was it actually good for me? I knew come Monday or Tuesday, I'd be sick from nerves. That's why I didn't ask for tomorrow—

Christoffe was talking.

I closed my eyes to concentrate on his French voice.

We set the date for the following Tuesday, at ten-thirty in the morning. "Morning is better for me," I said, because suddenly the words presented themselves, and I couldn't resist saying any complete phrase that came to mind no matter how inane, just to be able to speak a full sentence.

We were going to ring off. But I felt he needed more info about my hair. "I am a very blond blonde," I said

"Oui, Madame."

"But I am not a true blonde." Clarity was of the utmost importance here.

This time I was sure I heard a smile in his voice. "But of course, Madame."

I hung up and war danced around the apartment. Then I stopped. What was all that Madame business? How old did I sound on the phone anyway? And just what was that tone of voice about the trueness of my blond hair?

Then I wrote in my date book—"Christoffe. Tuesday, ten-thirty am…I think."

Tuesday dawned blustery and sunny. I sat straight up from sound sleep. "Damn hair."

I catered to my nerves by drinking less coffee than usual. I ate eggs and toast to calm me down even more. And set off.

The shop was in walking distance, and shortly, too shortly for my taste, I found myself standing across the street from it.

It was huge and looked very busy, very successful. Ladies and their dogs were going in and out. Obviously a popular place—

Relief swept in.

But then I double-checked the number. Wrong number.

My heart dropped. I looked again. I was certainly on the right street.

And then I saw it. There sat my shop, next door. A small shop. A mouse of a shop. Wasn't busy at all—

In fact it looked very closed for business. My heart dropped further.

But no. This was no time to panic, or even run. I looked more closely. And I saw that the storefront of my shop was not mousy, but rather, intensely minimalist. Some aluminum. Some bamboo. Some art deco lettering. It was silvery looking, as opposed to the popping place next door…which now that I was comparing it to my quietly chic little place, looked like Ethel Merman.

I stood on the opposite sidewalk, and as I watched, three women, two with dogs, hustled up to the loud, busy shop.

Mine sat there cool and calm displaying no signs of life, apparently above needing to be popular. Above needing more than one customer a day.

I hoped it wasn't scorned by the locals. I thought of my friend Natalie, a Yankee to her core, therefore careful with a penny…

I thought of Natalie's hair. It was gorgeous, thick and lustrous. I felt relief, because surely she pampered that hair with only the best.

But then I thought she doesn't need the best for that kind of hair. It could fend for itself. It was obvious that Natalie only needed to snap her fingers for it to spring into diva locks—

Or maybe it looked so good *because* Christoffe took care of it.

Get over there—

Because the bottom line was my roots were screaming. In honor of Halloween, that night I was going to a talk at the

American Library about hunting ghosts, given by the English ghost hunter Simon Marsden. I could not show up, intent on having conversations in English, with roots.

Still, not one woman had entered my silent jewel. No, they all seemed to crave the dive next door.

Maybe this was the wrong day/time/place on earth?

GET OVER THERE—

A discreet little bingle as I opened the door. A willowy young man turned around, and I beheld a face so unconsciously mournful and pale, he could only be French...or a therapist. I advanced diffidently, holding out my hand. When I spoke, it came out too loud. "Christoffe?"

He smiled a tired, forgiving smile. He nodded. His handshake was limp. If an American man shook my hand that way I'd slap his face. But this was Paris. The limp handshake appeared de rigueur. Maybe because they do so much more of it than we do.

So, I shook his hand. I murmured his name. He said, "Madame." Then he ushered me into my chair, and in an odd way, like just out of sight in another dimension, my date with the French hairdresser began.

I was indeed the only person in the shop. There were four chairs though. Maybe Tuesday at 10:30 a.m. was not favored by the clientele of this shop...although certainly the women next door were not so picky. Christoffe smiled gently enough but seemed the quiet type. I clutched the arms of the chair.

"Your color is good? You want the same color?"

DON'T MESS WITH THE COLOR, MISTER.

"Yes, I like the color. Very blond. Give me the same color, please," I said, my heart fluttering.

He rubbed his hands through my hair, holding it up to the light, the mirror, me, as if I could do something about it. Coached by Natalie, I said, "I am growing my hair to one length. So please cut very little." He nodded, a tiny smile touching the edge of his lips.

"Your hair is in good condition," he said. A Gallic shrug of his shoulders.

Praise be—

I didn't relax or anything. I'd practically used up my lexicon of hairdresser French. My armpits were sweating.

Christoffe put the apron around my neck. "I will be back." Maybe he was keeping his conversation to a minimum as a nod to my language difficulties?

I nodded. I pried my fingers off the arm of the chair.

The door bingled, opened, and a dark man exuding energy came in. There was an infinitesimal stop…then he and Christoffe nodded at each other.

Silence. When one loses a sense, the others pick up. So now, having lost the ability to speak, my nerves picked up the unspoken vibes. Christoffe and the man were having a fight…a domestic one.

The man strode over and introduced himself. Joseph. He was a whirlwind of fresh air. Christoffe and he owned the shop together, he told me. Happy to have you here, he said, grinning. I wondered how he could possibly be a Parisian with a grin like that.

Christoffe barely looked at him. Joseph gave a quick look toward Christoffe, and saw that yes, Christoffe was not speaking to him.

So, being supremely sure of his rightness, Joseph backed off.

Christoffe came up and began applying my color.

I needed to talk. I didn't know what to stare at if I wasn't going to be able to talk. The mirror was huge. All I could look at was either my face or his.

I really needed to talk. It was instinctual. After going to the hairdressers for forty years, this was the result. Hairdresser talk. Like Pavlov's dog.

For a moment it was total silence. There wasn't even music. There weren't even other customers chattering. There wasn't even Joseph—

I wanted to say, so how's it going with Joseph? He seems louder than usual. Is he still refusing to go to therapy with you? And you. How's your spleen? How's your mother and that hated sister of yours? How's your dog—

A light bulb.

"Do you have a dog?" I asked, since I couldn't very well open up the conversation with "So, how long have you and Joseph been together?"

"No," he said. "No dog."

"I have a cat," I said. "She's very sad I'm here in Paris."

"Ah yes, it is so with cats. They miss people."

"Do you have a cat?"

"I had a cat, but she died two years ago."

I clucked, but inwardly I exulted. We were talking!

"Oh, I'm sorry. How old was she?"

"She was sixteen. Her name was Anna."

"Sixteen. Wow. That's an old cat."

Silence fell.

No. No more silence. Not for me.

"Do you want another cat?"

He shook his head sorrowfully. "I still miss Anna too much for another cat."

Well, maybe he should get another one, anyway. Might take

his mind off Joseph's transgressions. Joseph was definitely not the pet sort. Or had an odd pet compulsion, like a python, say, which drove the orderly Christoffe crazy, especially as Joseph insisted it be allowed to sleep with them when it was cold, because everyone knows that pythons feel the cold terribly.

If Christoffe had understood English I could have told him that pythons don't get cold, but they're deaf, so he could call it all sorts of names, and the python would never know.

I moved us onto siblings, children (mine), mothers (his), and where he was from. It turned out that he was from Normandy, but had lived in Paris for twenty years and therefore considered himself a Parisian by now.

Politely he asked me where I was from. I said Los Angeles because I figured it was easier to place than Newport Beach.

A lapse into silence. But even I needed a rest. Out of the corner of my eye I saw a parade of people trod by the shop's huge windows in the front. The word for "window" popped unbidden into my head—

"Your *fenetres* are beautiful. So much to see—"

He lit up. Suddenly I could see the man Joseph had fallen in love with. "Ah yes, the windows. We just had them put in last year. Thank god for the windows. It felt like a prison in here before."

"Beautiful," I said, my voice dripping with appreciation—

Dripping with relief too. Because the color was done. The need for extended conversation was at an end. Now I'd simply sit underneath the dryer. Then during the trim and styling I wouldn't utter a peep, the better to let him concentrate.

My god. May I nap now?

As I was paying, another customer finally came in. An

elderly woman with carrot-colored hair. Her hair was totally awry, dirty, and unbrushed. But she was beaming. She was bustling. *"Hallo, M. Christoffe. Bonjour."* She dragged a tiny pug in behind her. The wind slammed the door shut. "I'll just sit and wait over here, *cher* Christoffe," she trilled. The pug yelped in unison.

Christoffe smiled at me and rolled his eyes. The shrug of his shoulders said she was a dear. The pug continued yapping, Madame shushing half-heartedly. Christoffe rolled his eyes again.

Then, something came over me. I couldn't help it. My hair had turned out this side of fabulous. What can I say? I was beyond relieved. I was beyond grateful. Because of M. Christoffe here, I could hold my head high at the American Library later that night. *"Merci, M. Christoffe,"* I trilled.

I moved toward him, and as he realized my very American intention, his face paled in consternation—

I hugged M. Christoffe.

BLOWN TO BITS

Parisian women are the epitome of chic. This is a fact even two-year-olds know.

Parisian women and their windblown, I'm-too-sultry-to-give-a-damn hair. The fabulous tailored overcoat slung shut with that belt. Those scarves, looking like they flung themselves around their necks on the run, but no, darlings, they did not. It must be learned at Maman's knee—

I know this because I was in a scarf shop one day. Such fantastic scarves. I should have just been looking, but then I couldn't stop myself. Even under the hawk-like eyes of the saleswoman, whose total demeanor screamed, "Don't touch, you American cretin," I pulled one off the dowel to which it had been tied so chicly. I tried it on. But alas, it didn't look as good on me as it did on the dowel. So I tried to retie it onto that pale wood dowel. I thought I'd remembered from when I'd untied it three seconds before.

Impossible. I tried two, three, almost four times, to do it right, when the sales madame glided like a cobra to my side, snatching the scarf from my hopeless manipulations. She retied it with élan. *"Voila, Madame,"* she cooed coolly, *"comme ça."* She did not deign to look at me, or perhaps she was trying to spare me further embarrassment. Quickly I was outside in the bracing air, sans any kind of new scarf.

Parisian women are cruel to their feet. They wear killer boots, and clatter down the sidewalk like they've never heard of rubber tips on heels and soles. They walk very fast. They approach from behind, clacking loudly, and then tailgate until the first possible moment when they can rush around you.

I walk fast. And I'm competitive. I hate a tailgater too, although usually my ire occurs on Californian freeways. So my goal is to walk faster. Which I should be able to do because I am *not* wearing boots with toes so narrow they could slice tomatoes. I'm wearing shoes with rubber soles.

But I cannot.

Maybe they can do this to their feet because there are huge sections in the pharmacies devoted to foot care. Sophisticated foot care all devoted to helping the bunions, the calluses, the blisters, the sprained toe, the sprained ankle, the bruised soles of the feet. When my friend Natalie showed me these products, I felt like I was a peeping Tom at a foot fetish bazaar.

Parisian women wear their eye makeup smudged like they wear it to bed—

Lipstick? Hah. For plebeians and foreigners.

So I thought it took time to achieve this unstudied take-my-tendril-and-smudged-mascara look. I thought it was on purpose—

Like my own California casual chic takes time. *Mais oui!*

But, *mais non.* These women have adapted to their harsh environment so perfectly they have turned their daily lives into a style the rest of the world holds as the epitome of chic. The windblown, I-Just-Got-Out-of-Bed look.

This look has come to be because of one simple fact. Parisian women walk everywhere.

They are out in the elements every day being blown to bits. Hence the reddened face that doesn't need lipstick.

They are out on city sidewalks, teeming with other people, and wind. Those belted coats and luxurious scarves hiding, therefore, the need for an expensive outfit underneath, allowing them to focus their stash of euros on the belt, the scarf, the superb coat. They use the metro, which is vicious. One walks through a cyclone, a wind tunnel, each and every time one enters or exits the metro. Hence the tousled hair, omigod, that sexy hair.

I walk nowhere in California. I *go* for a walk. I *take* a walk. But in the course of my daily life, I do not leave my front door and walk to my destination. Ever.

It was a major adjustment, all this walking. I was exposed to the elements in a manner to which I was not accustomed. It's one thing to go outside for fresh air. It is another thing to leave my front door coifed to the hilt, not a tendril out of place, and be met with the full fury of Mother Nature at street level, on foot.

One toe over the threshold, and my hair was blown to bits. Each and every day. Without fail.

It pissed me off. Each and every day.

Because not only was I out on a sidewalk, it was a Parisian sidewalk, which meant it was full of clacking heels and tailgaters; it meant it was a six-block walk to my metro. It was always a six-block walk to my metro, no matter where I stayed.

Then, upon reaching the metro in a state of windblown

madness, I descended into the bowels of the metro, where my hair, coat, and scarf met still another assault to my person, the metro's own version of madness—the wind tunnel, the wind cyclone, the shrieking blizzard of wind. Maybe there's a cute Gallic name for this phenomenon. I don't know it, yet.

By the time I was standing (still standing, not lounging behind the wheel of my car) on the platform waiting for the actual metro itself, I was a ragged version of what I had been not twenty minutes before, in the calm of my apartment.

At first I thought my bedraggled appearance was my hair's fault. My hair does not do windblown. It's fine. It's shortish. It's picky and difficult to deal with.

I'd learned to counter these difficulties with a Marilyn Monroe blonde, but in the face of being outside, on actual sidewalks, every day for hours on end, my hair quit.

As for clothes? My California staples fell by the wayside too—

Baseball hats? Omigod.

Running shoes? Let's not even go there.

Sunglasses. No one wore them. Was it because the sun wasn't there all that much, so that when it was, everyone chose to expose their eyeballs to the color sun brought to their dark city?

The women, while eschewing lipstick, wore huge amounts of eye makeup. Maybe that's why there were no sunglasses. I wore sunglasses because I wore no eye makeup—

I wore lipstick, though. Even though no one else did. If I saw a woman wearing lipstick, I knew immediately she was from somewhere else, or had an American mother hidden in her closet.

But I was there to adapt. To fit in. Best I could, anyway.

So I stowed the red baseball cap from Beijing and the running shoes from Runner's World in my suitcase.

I kept the sunglasses, but wore them as infrequently as possible.

I toned down the lipstick and started wearing eye makeup.

I wore my black shoes everywhere, except for the few times I brought out my chocolate suede boots or my sky-blue heels. These could only be used when the outing was to be short, and if I thought I would still be able to walk in them by the time I had to climb that last flight of metro stairs, negotiate the six-block walk home, and finally crawl up the four flights to my apartment.

The first trip I wore the chocolate suede boots three times, the heels not at all.

The second trip I wore the boots once, and the heels once.

The third trip they both stayed at home. I brought only my faithful Mephistos, newly aided by a matching pair in brown. I figured if I were to suddenly find myself with a diplomatic ball to go to, I'd shop and damn the cost.

I knew how to live.

By the third trip I had recovered my sanity. I realized as much as I wanted to be a good American in Paris, I didn't want to deny what worked for me. So I went back to my lipstick, and quit eye makeup.

Nonetheless, the windblown issue never let up. Stepping out the door every day, to walk and walk and walk, that first gust of wind would hit, and my mood was fried.

It wasn't until the third trip that my hair and I learned how to be at one with windblown.

One day my flat-iron died, once again. I had ultimately replaced it on that first trip, buying a new one at a different Monoprix across town. And this French *lisseur* had accompanied me on trip two, and now it was day fifteen, trip three. I plugged it in, just like every day, and it failed to light up. I looked at the French flat-iron and knew defeat. I threw it away.

I looked at my hair in the mirror. I have what is politely called "wavy" hair. This actually means you can't do anything with it, but never mind.

It was curled up on the top of my head (like it was every morning) looking like Shirley Temple before they added all those fake curls. In the back, my hair waved anemically.

But man, the color shone. The red lipstick was demanding attention. The tailored coat covering the basic outfit, and the French scarf I now knew how to sling, were doing their job. The black shoes? They were so right they cried for joy.

So I said to hell with it. You and me, hair, I said, we're going out just like this because we do not care what zee others will think about it. Besides, zee top curls are *tres* cute, *n'est pas?*

Oui, cherie.

Eh bien—

I stepped out the door and the wind blew me and my hair to bits.

But, the natural curls on the top of my head withstood the assault. The rest of my hair, nudged into action, curled in sympathy. And in one moment (I know because I checked in a store window) my hair took on that just-got-out-of-bed look.

And so, I found out how come the Parisians always look

so pulled together in spite of the windblown you-know-what. It's all natural. *Eh bien*, who knew?

After that I challenged the wind to have its way with my hair. Because I had finally learned that the secret to chic in living in a wind tunnel is to ignore it.

EXACT CHANGE

The day I paid for my *International Herald* with the exact change, I fully expected fireworks. Because paying with the exact change made me a native. It had required serious study. It was, in my book, the outer stratosphere of accomplishment.

I was driven to it.

I dreaded money transactions. For one thing, I never understood the amount of euros when the salesperson said it. "Euro" is an odd-sounding word spoken in French. It sounds more like "urine" than anything else. It requires a ferocious pursing of the lips while being spoken, and while the French speak their lovely language with a huge amount of lip pursing already, even they need to amp it up to get around pronouncing "euro."

So, the amount would be spoken, and I would make a frantic attempt to extract the number word from "urine." Then I would produce bills that I hoped were somewhat close to the number I thought I'd heard. But I was always asked for smaller bills or different coins. I'd come to dread the bland gaze of the salesperson shaking her head, returning my bill. "Something *plus petit*?" she'd say, holding out her hand, gazing darkly off into the distance, waiting. I'd grown tired of the flash of panic. *What* was she saying? I was sick of being capable only of going mute, the wind knocked out of my sails, reduced now to offering up a wad of bills, or a palmful of change by way of apology. She'd lean forward, strict-looking and weary, to choose what she needed.

I'd arrived in Paris determined to show them an American could be just as good a Parisian as anyone. To that effect, I had made gargantuan efforts, while throwing my money around, to knowing how much I was spending—

But it gradually became clear to me that mentally translating every euro I spent into dollars and cents, although a personal apex in mathematical acumen, would not suffice.

So, I challenged myself to learn the coins. And I upped the ante. I would learn to recognize them without my reading glasses—

Hunting the depths of my purse for my reading glasses had become another hair-raiser. Although this issue had already arrived without invitation a few years ago in the safety of America, it really stressed me out in Paris. I have no intention of becoming one of those doddering old women who stop the world while they hunt through their purses looking for whatever. Here in Paris, overnight, I became one of those women every time I needed something out of my purse. Like the damn wallet…like the change out of the wallet.

It had become a serious matter of saving face.

I started small. I dumped all my change on the bed, and separated out the biggest coin. It was the two-euro coin. I memorized it. Okay, that was easy. It was the biggest coin. Like a two-dollar coin.

Emboldened, I added the one-euro coin. It was the next in size. Still pretty big, and not easily confused with the next smaller coin, the fifty centime. These two coins, then, became the only coins I carried in my wallet. All the other change was left in the apartment, on the tiny mantel in my bedroom, in a small green dish.

For a while this sufficed, more for my ego than anything else, because I continued to be asked for more precise change. So soon I was driven to add the fifty-centime piece. Two days later, in a gesture of grandiosity, and after much practice there in my bedroom, I added the twenty- and the ten-centime coins. This was the day I paid for the *International Herald* with exact change.

The kiosk man did not rear back in amazement. He could have. I'd been getting my newspaper and magazines there often enough. He could have. There isn't a Frenchman alive who isn't part Maurice Chevalier.

The woman before me had simply held out her purse for him to help himself. She was even French, speaking French and everything, and I watched as he indulgently pulled out the right coins. She was elderly and tired looking, so maybe that was enough of an excuse. Or maybe she'd left her reading glasses at home. Of course I certainly empathized.

I watched her let the kiosk man do all the work, feeling smug.

I surreptitiously checked the coins in my fist again. There was a one-euro coin, four twenty-centime coins, and two ten centimes.

The elderly woman took her time stepping out of the way. I wanted to lift her bodily out of the way. I could have. She was tiny. I would have been kind about it. I would have issued a shove masquerading as a friendly pat, murmured, "Bonjour, Madame," caught her elbow as she missed the step, steadied her, and smiled benignly at the white tendrils escaping her bun as she tottered away.

Finally it was my turn. The kiosk man lifted his left eyebrow by way of saying, *"Bonjour, Madame.* Don't you look fab today." They seem to have learned this in their cradles.

I held up my *International Herald.* I smiled. A halo singed my hair. He said, *"Deux euros, Madame."* ("Two urines, Madame.")

I dumped the coins into his palm, needing to shake the last centime loose, the little sucker. I cast a casual look at his face.

He didn't even look at the coins. He accepted them like it wouldn't have mattered what I handed him. That he would have indulgently accepted whatever mishmash of coin I'd tossed his way. He smiled at me. He was being kind to the foreign lady.

I searched my vocabulary. As usual, under duress it disappeared. *"La change, c'est…*er…*correct?"*

He looked surprised. *"Oui, oui, Madame."* He threw my perfect selection of coins into the cash register. He directed his gaze to the man behind me.

What did I want?

Okay, I wanted a medal.

It was dusk. The sky was pewter and pink. The clouds were thin and soft. No fireworks? *Tant pis.* I shrugged a Gallic shrug. I stepped down the little step. I pushed a tendril behind my ear. I couldn't have been more French than Catherine Deneuve.

I crossed over the Alma Marceau bridge. The Eiffel Tower stood calm in the quiet light. It was the time of day everyone was going home. I hung over the wall of the bridge and watched two *bateaux mouches* pass, full of tourists who didn't care whether or not they paid with the correct change. But they were only here for five days. They did not have the time.

I had the time. I had the extravagance of time.

And I had paid with the exact change for the first time ever.

The breeze was lovely. I hastened on. I was headed for the boulangerie to buy dinner. A tomato and bacon quiche sounded good. And that cost two euros, a fifty-centime coin, and two ten centimes—

Which I had.

THE GREEN BENCHES
OF PARIS

You've seen them. They are all over Paris, ubiquitous to the extreme, except they are so goddamn picturesque, why not strew them all over the place?

I refer to Paris's green park benches. Like straight out of 1895.

The very first day I was in Paris, I sheepishly snuck a Starbucks over to what turned out to be on Île de la Cité. I spied one of those green benches, oh so French looking, eagerly hastened over to it, and tried to sit down to enjoy my coffee and the big, gold-tinted buildings in front of me. They turned out to be the Palais de Justice, and my green bench was in the Place de Lepine, but at that moment, jet lag still lurking, I was simply enthralled I was breathing Parisian air, and was, like magic, like flying carpet magic, so far away from Newport Beach, California.

But, I couldn't get comfortable. I couldn't figure how on earth one was supposed to sit on the sharply angled slats of the bench. It had looked innocuous enough as I aimed my rear end downward. But when I hit the bench,

I practically slid right through, leaving my knees up under my chin.

I felt a nudge of irritation. Were these darling green benches going to turn out to be all looks and no comfort? My old dislike of Paris threatened to emerge…until I shut the door on my twelve-year-old self and squirmed for comfort, since no one else seemed to be having any problem here.

In fact a woman was sitting on the other end of my bench, and she wasn't having any problems with it. No. It was her child she was having problems with, judging from the tone of voice in which she was saying *"Cherie."* Also, I heard key words like *professeur* and *l'école*, which led me to believe that her darling child had been the subject of a school conference Maman had just attended, and she wasn't happy with what the teachers had said.

This was a busy working mother, on a quick break, sitting on the bench, purse, keys, coffee cup, and scarf all in motion, lowering the boom on the kid. No problem with this awkward bench.

Later the green benches became as comfortable as my black shoes. But this was only after I learned how to open the park gates.

There are small parks on every corner of Paris, and these neighborhood parks have gates. I wanted in, as a respite from the harrowing chockfull sidewalks of Paris, but at first the mechanism threw me. In fact it seemed like maybe the park was closed, because oftentimes there weren't any people within. Maybe these parks were closed to the motley public. So that thought allowed me to feel deprived and singled out by the Parisian powers that be.

But then I'd see people in these little parks, sitting quietly on the green benches, reading or eating. Maybe using their cells. Taking a bit of air and nature amidst the din of the city. Inside these parks it was always quiet.

Well, I wanted to take a leafy respite, but first I had to figure out how to open the damn gate—

Doors and gates in Paris need to be mastered. You have been warned—

So the first trip I skipped all parks that required gate opening. It had been harrowing enough to learn the ins and outs of door opening on the metro. It had been difficult getting the hang of my apartment door.

But by the second trip I was ready to claim my place in the little city parks of Paris.

Of course the gates were simple as pie, when I finally put my mind to it. Maybe some Parisian was infiltrating my DNA?

Once the parks were open to me there wasn't a park I didn't go into.

One day I was in the Marais. I'd just done the Carnavalet and the Picasso museums. I was walking down a narrow sidewalk when along came a park. I slipped in for a bit of solitude.

Once off the cobblestone street, it was instantly quiet. This one, called Square Charles V Langlois, was sided by the solid walls of buildings, and had a straightforward, bare bones attitude. It consisted of one path circling the oval shape. There was green grass in the middle, and tall trees around the edges. The green benches. *C'est tout.*

I walked to the end farthest away from the street. There were two benches back there, under the trees. On close inspection, one was liberally sprinkled with bird droppings.

I sat down on the other one. In the silence, Picasso's cross-eyed paintings clanged in my brain. I closed my eyes and listened to the peace. I felt spiritual. I pulled out my notebook to write about peace and spirituality amidst the medieval sprawl that is Le Marais, even though my brain muttered, "Just be."

Pen poised over paper I looked around myself, and saw that there was writing on the infested bench.

Graffiti? In here? How do they find it? Have they no shame? The "they" being any young person carrying a knapsack and wearing an expensive watch.

I got up to see what it said, even though again, my spiritual self implored I just sit and get on with the peace.

I got up anyway, but I needed my reading glasses. Okay, so this was turning into a big deal because I couldn't find my glasses until I pulled out the extra sweater, the brochures from both museums, until I moved aside my sunglasses. My never used sunglasses.

Finally, underneath my wallet, there they were, so very Prada. I slipped them on. I leaned in to read the writing scratched into the green paint on the back of the bench. Underneath the words was an arrow pointing down to the emissions.

The words were "FREE NATURE."

Ha! Yeah. Good one. In English too. Funny.

I sat back down on my bench and felt beatific and smugly safe. *My* bench was clear. *My* bench was clean. Apparently the birds didn't like my bench. How clever of them. How nice for me.

Birds flapped through the trees—

Wait a minute…

Birds have no compunction. Birds have no brains. Birds don't pick one bench over the other.

It seemed like more birds were flapping through the trees overhead—

I beat a hasty retreat.

STE. CHAPELLE EST FERMÉ

I was walking across the Île de la Cité on my way home. I was thinking about that long-ago day when I was fresh off the plane, sitting right here, sheepishly drinking a Starbucks. I was admiring the Palais de Justice (not knowing what it was), even as I wondered how anyone managed to sit on the green park benches all over Paris. I thought I was on the Left Bank—

Now I knew different.

Now I was cutting across to use a new and different metro. This would be another chance to pat myself on the back with how comfortable I had gotten using them. How my metro instincts were kicking in and starting to point me in the right direction. How sometimes, even, I just knew the right metro without having to double-check three million times before descending to the bowels of Paris.

As I walked I realized I was walking by Ste. Chapelle. I slowed down. My father had strongly recommended I get in to see the gorgeous windows…but I'd already seen two museums today, which was way outside my comfort zone when it came to museums. This meant I was tired and had

had enough. I was going home this way to check out the different metro.

But a buzz of *yes I can* coursed through my sightseeing veins, and I knew I could do it. This would make three cultural events and one ride on a new metro line in one day. For the short-attention-span tourist, this meant it had been a day of sightseeing triumph!

There was a line waiting to go in. Not good. Not good at all. Lines are monsters. They rip one's sense of well-being to shreds.

And this was a church. There aren't supposed to be lines to go into churches, for god's sake—

My thoughts immediately turned to my apartment. The fresh sugar bread and ham and cheese from Bon Marche coming to room temperature. The *International Herald* waiting. The exceptional couch and its red throw just waiting for me to kick off the black shoes and settle down for a quiet evening in my ragged sweats, reveling in a day well spent.

But I pulled myself together. What's a line, I thought. I can do this.

So I trudged over, and just as I was about to plant myself dutifully in place, a tired-looking woman, her nose brooking no argument, came out of Ste. Chapelle and, seemingly quite arbitrarily, plunked down a sign. She did not plunk this sign down at the beginning of the line. Nor did she plunk it right behind me, the last one in line. No. She plunked it down right in the middle of the lines, brushing people out of the way to do so. She plunked it down right in front of two couples obviously traveling together. They looked like American college professors. There were about twenty people in line in front of them. And about fifteen, me included, behind them.

The sign said *"Ste. Chapelle est fermé."* And as she set it down right in the middle of the line, she announced in that high singsong voice the French acquire when they know the news isn't good...for you: *"Ste. Chapelle est fermé."* She did not bother to repeat this in English, or German or Italian for that matter.

The two couples upon whose feet the sign had been placed didn't believe it. "I don't believe it," they said. "Do you believe it?" they said, looking at each other in dignified amazement. There was also a disturbed rustle from the others behind them.

I, too, went into denial. How could the place be closed? It was only 3:30 p.m.

And what was up with this rudeness with the sign placement?

People began to disperse. Except the American couples, who were still standing there, stunned. How could this be? They had *already* been in line—

Which somewhere else might have meant something.

Now they were angry. The Frenchwoman didn't care. She repeated the bad news, shaking her head, fending off their indignant questions. *"Ste. Chapelle est fermé."* Shoved the sign a little closer to them to emphasize her point.

Me? I heard those words and I knew. I knew there would be no more Ste. Chapelle today.

But I needed to ask her a question. "Eet eez closed," she was saying to the American man, who still thought his incredulous tone of voice would somehow change the situation. Yeah, well, I knew better.

"Madame," I called out, showing off a little. Because I doubt the Americans had used the word "madame" once. She turned and saw another American, and started to shake her head wearily. *"Madame,"* I said, so politely, *"ou est le metro Cité? La bas?"* I gestured to where I thought it was. Now I was just a tired American who needed to get to the metro.

"Ah oui, Madame. La bas," she said, and managed a small smile.

Gold! A smile from a Frenchwoman closing down the Ste. Chapelle in the face of peeved tourists.

I smirked all the way to the station.

I threw my ticket in, and scarcely looking where I was going, because I knew the basics like I knew my ten toes, I stepped where I was supposed to be, and the doors slid shut. I was trapped in an elevator going down, and I was alone.

Never, ever smirk. Never feel superior to one's own countrymen. Never think you know it all.

Because I sure had never heard of an elevator in a metro. And I feared to loathing elevators.

It was huge, like a cattle call elevator, like a grain elevator. Nothing is huge in Paris, particularly elevators.

Why was there suddenly an elevator in a metro? What would these diabolical Frenchmen come up with next?

The elevator moved extremely quietly, as well. Almost didn't feel like it was moving at all—

I was suddenly panicked. I was suddenly very sorry for having felt smug—

So, I prayed in this elevator.

I would rush right back, if I were ever released from this godforsaken contraption, and make amends for my smugness by punching out the Frenchwoman for closing down Ste. Chapelle just when my very own American brothers and sisters, who had their hearts set on seeing it, and indeed planned to pay worshipful homage to it, and even make

anti-American remarks while doing so, like "There's nothing as beautiful as this in America," who probably only had
a week in her city and were probably spending more money
in this week, ill-fated now, reeking with failure now, than
she earned in a year, and which paid her salary there at Ste.
Chapelle.

Was that proper gratitude from that Frenchwoman, even
if she had smiled at me?

Yes, maybe I would go back and have a hard word with
that self-righteous Parisian. And I would too, if I got out of
this elevator alive—

Which really worried me, because why was there even
an elevator here? Something wasn't right. Something was
very wrong, this elevator showing up right in my smugness-
ridden path.

How did I know I hadn't maybe died, and like in those
awful movies depicting what happens after death, millions
of people riding trains or escalators, all on their confused
way to the Pearly Gates, this was exactly what was happening to me now?

This was payback time, big-time, for every smug moment
I'd ever had in Paris, and indeed throughout a life riddled
with smug moments, and I hereby wanted to tell God, no,
beg God for mercy. I was hereby promising God, if He ever
let me off this godforsaken elevator, I would never, ever be
smug again. Instead I would count my blessings every moment of every day, and praise the good Lord, who gave me
Paris in the first place, if He would please, please, please
spare me now—

The doors slid open, and there was a waiting metro, going in the right direction.

WALKING
THROUGH THE TUILERIES

The bell-ringing concert at Église St. Germain l'Auxerrois had been calling me since I'd first heard about it. So this was the day I'd get there if it killed me. It was at 3:30 in the afternoon on Wednesdays, a perfectly benign day of the week, a perfectly benign time of day. This should have been oh so doable. But I hadn't managed to pull it off yet, no matter how much I intended.

I emerged from the metro at the Place de la Concorde, a huge, frantic traffic circle, the queen of traffic circles. I had given myself enough time to stroll through the Tuileries to get there.

I ran up the stairs to the Tuileries and came face to face with the Galerie du Jeu de Paume. It's so stately, sitting there all by itself, looking most beguiling. It had been closed for renovations on my first trip. I'd had to make do with staring at it longingly.

But now it was open. Renovations finished. Now it was a gallery for photography. I love photography. And the main exhibit was Edward Steichen. I love Edward Steichen's work.

So how could I pass this opportunity up?

I stepped in—

To find the seventeenth-century building had become a brand-new, modern, gleaming white ode to the twenty-first century. It was a profusion of perfect gallery-speak white walls, black-and-white photography, and even a sleek escalator right up the middle. I almost left, but the entry fee was reasonable. And...Steichen beckoned.

I rode up the escalator to Steichen, and found the man had been a photo fiend, with eight million photographs to show for it, and the Jeu de Paume had hung every single one of them. The white walls were alive with miniscule black-and-white photos looking like an invasion of ants.

Dutifully I got out my reading glasses and made a stab at appearing to pore over each and every one of them. In five minutes I was done. What was there to discover? Eight million moments of genius? Too much. I wanted to leave. But I'd only been there five minutes. I try to stay in a museum (or certainly a remodeled photo gallery) twenty minutes. To show some cultural awareness. To show some manners. But, but—

Then I espied Steichen's fashion photography. Well, I love fashion photography.

So now I lingered happily, bell concert be damned. His work was truly stunning. And then I came to a little space where they were showing a video of Steichen actually at work. How fascinating, *n'est pas*? I settled in happily. There he was. Photographing a beautiful model in a gauzy ball gown. All froth and delicate beauty. He moved the model here and there, her arm slung this way, her head tilted that way. He spoke to his various assistants. He peered into various cameras. But?

But he had a cigar clenched between his teeth. In that pristine-seeming set, he was billowing smoke. He was 1880 London. He was fog and dirt on a dreary night. He was toxic.

The smoke was everywhere. I choked. The smoking on the streets of Paris was already unbelievable. And now I was getting it inside a pure white gallery?

Gasping for air, I fled.

Outside it was cool and gray. I gulped in huge breaths as I hastened down to the wide center path and ran right into a bigger-than-god Ferris wheel. It loomed over the Tuileries. It loomed over the world. It beckoned—

But was I in Paris to ride on a Ferris wheel? Ever since that first time I was on a Ferris wheel, when I was three, with my father, and the thing broke and we were stuck at the top for way too long, and it started to rain—

I am leery of them. But this one would be worth it. The view of the Eiffel Tower from it had to be fabulous, right?

But I was a little late. I'd be royally pissed if I were late for the bell-ringing concert at Église St. Germain l'Auxerrois.

I ripped myself away.

And ran right into gardeners for the Tuileries putting the gorgeous flower beds down for the winter.

There were two gardeners. They were leaning on their rakes as I passed, the history of Paris their backdrop. I felt a peaceful kind of envy. These two men worked with history and nature every day. That night they would go to the café, and over beer someone would ask them what they did for a living. One gardener wouldn't deign to reply. The other, loquacious after the fourth beer, would say, "I'm a gardener at the Tuileries."

"Does it pay?" the stupid upstart would ask.

"Of course not. I do it for the love of France and all this great country means to me." The young guy would purse his lips, tug thoughtfully at his scarf. His iPhone would blare electronic dissonance. *"Eh bien, bon,"* he'd mutter, his attention already diverted by the sparkling phone.

On the wide steps leading up to the street to cross over to the Louvre was a gaggle of pre-teenagers, on a school outing. They were sitting in a motley group, waiting for the next step.

Last time I'd passed by here there was a younger group of schoolchildren, and a couple of little boys had come running up to the group waving bouquets they'd obviously scalped from the gardens. I expected a huge outcry from the teachers, but no. Then I saw. All the students had motley bouquets of flowers too.

Not this bunch today. They were almost teenagers, and had already found out that a few euros would buy a ready-made bouquet. Although they weren't at the age where they needed to be buying flowers.

Not yet.

But life is long, and life isn't necessarily fair, and as I looked at the twelve-year-old boys in the group, I knew that each and every one of them, at some time in their future, would need to buy a bouquet of flowers, and each of those girls was going to receive it and have to decide for herself if she was willing to believe his cockamamie story.

But okay, so now I was running late. It's a totally different experience being late on foot than in a car. I should have started to run, but this was Paris. I was a grown woman. Running was out of the question.

And then some pink-cheeked upstart, sucking on a lollipop, obviously late too, ran by me, his school tie flapping

in the wind. Lucky for both the kid and me, I couldn't come
up with enough French words to shout at him to stop running
with a godforsaken lollipop in his mouth.

Didn't matter. Because voila! There was l'Église St.
Germain l'Auxerrois.

I jay-walked it across the cobblestones, hauled open the
venerable doors, and lurched in, out of breath and panting,
to find—

There was to be no bell-ringing concert today.

Instead there was to be…construction.

It seemed a major renovation was in progress. The main
altar was cordoned off, and many men were on their knees
installing a new floor.

How could it be possible to replace an ancient floor in an
ancient cathedral? New wiring? New plumbing? Removing
a long-forgotten casket?

I was outraged. No warning. No signs posted, begging
my forgiveness for no bell ringing. Would that have been
too much? Do they also let one wallow on the expressways,
only posting the signs to the exits as the innocent driver sails
by in the left lane? I could have killed. Paris can do that to
a person.

I should have gotten on that Ferris wheel. I could have
stopped for pistachio ice cream, although it was getting a little cold. I could have engaged the gardeners, where I would
have attempted to do better for myself than the twerp in the
bar.

No bell ringing. Again…

Breathe.

I teetered over to my favorite statue, sat down, and began self-righteously attempting to pray a humble (I hoped)
prayer of thanks for all I did have, when an old woman, bent

over her cane, hobbled slowly up to my statue and began the arduous process of lighting a candle. She positioned herself between me and my ardent prayer.

This was the last straw.

I rose like an avenging angel, intending to grab her scruffy neck and throw her out of my life. But upon standing I saw she barely came to my waist. Her gnarled hand shook as she held the match to the candle. The glow of the candles lit her solemn face, and she was so lost in her own prayers she didn't even notice I was there.

I departed quietly.

Outside it was now windy and getting colder by the minute. It felt good.

I took the metro home. Once there, I stopped at the kiosk for my daily newspaper. I went into Paul's for brioche and some croissants. I stepped across the tiny street and picked up tomatoes and mushrooms. I hit the dreaded grocery store for eggs, paper towels, and jam. The line was not bad. The cashier loved my exact change.

Loaded down now with my daily purchases, I got to my building. I pressed in my code. The door clicked and I pushed in. I went through the courtyard to the stairs. I climbed four flights of stairs. I shuffled through my very large bag and found my key, which was where it was supposed to be. I put the key in my door. It swung open, and I entered my home away from home. I turned up the heat, tore off a hunk of brioche, sank down onto my couch, and opened the newspaper.

MOTORCYCLES, THE HIDDEN THREAT

Crossing the street I checked for motorcycles more carefully than I did for speeding busses. Motorcyclists are everywhere, even on the sidewalks in certain parts of town. They appear to have a huge sense of entitlement, coupled with just enough hostility to keep me on the alert.

Maybe this is because they get no respect when they're down.

I was having a coffee and apricot tart one early afternoon with an acquaintance, when right in front of my eyes I saw one of those pesky motorcyclists get hit by a car...a tiny car, yes, but a car nonetheless...and the motorcyclist was sent flying.

I choked on the tart, tried to stand up, stammering to the person I was with, "Omigod, did you see that?" He nodded, not moving an inch.

"Is he all right? Shouldn't we do something?"

He pursed his lips, smiled indulgently, and patted my knee. "Zees happens all zee time."

"All the time?" My gaze snuck back to the tragedy unfolding before my very eyes.

"All zee time. It's nothing. He's okay. You will see," said my French friend. He resumed drinking his coffee, and obviously the conversation was supposed to resume where it left off.

Meanwhile people were kneeling and hovering around the fallen motorcyclist. I couldn't tell which one was the driver of the car, but certainly the car was uninjured.

Everything did indeed seem to be under control. There was no screaming. Dutifully I returned to the conversation.

Later...a different trip later...I was walking down Ave. George V, again engaged in an engaging conversation, when I witnessed a repeat of the above.

Only this time the motorcyclist didn't fall. The driver of the car who hit him did.

She leapt out of the car the minute she saw what she had wrought, but instead of running to the man she'd mowed down, she ran in little circles right by her car, wringing her hands. She wore very large sunglasses, she was very tall, very thin, and in spite of it being a cool day, dressed in a sleeveless tank top. Her skirt was tight, but it was long and plaid. Whoever is behind this constantly recurring fad for plaid didn't spend fourteen years in school uniforms.

Anyway, she appeared to be weeping, or at least appeared to be trying to weep.

Then her running puttered to a halt. She clasped her face and collapsed in a graceful faint. "She's down," exclaimed my friend.

"She's faking it," I said. Suddenly I was sure. "Did you ever see such a dainty faint?" Real faints are messy and contorted. And one usually smashes their head. "Look," I said. "Her head is carefully nestled in her arms. Her legs are politely together rather than sprawled apart. She's not even twitching."

"You're hard," said my friend.

Dutifully people converged on the girl on the ground. They began splashing her face with bottled water. "That'll get her. It'll ruin her makeup."

The girl sat up abruptly, shoving the water throwers away. She began to wail loudly. "That doesn't sound like someone coming out of a dead faint," said my friend.

"You're getting the picture," I said.

"She probably works down the street at Dior in between auditioning for acting jobs," said my friend. "That's the company car, and now she's in trouble...unless she keeps crying."

The girl wailed louder as she was lifted to her feet.

Meanwhile, the motorcyclist who'd been hit? He was on his phone. To the police? His lawyer? Maman? Nobody was paying any attention to him, but several young boys were hovering over the fallen motorcycle.

"All seems under control," I said. My friend concurred.

We continued on down the street.

RUGBY

Gradually penetrating even my obliviousness to anything other than the Seine, the Eiffel Tower, the metro at Louvre Rivoli, and where they hid Comet at the grocery store, I became aware of a growing tide of sports hysteria.

Rugby was coming to town, and I mean on a golden platter. It was the International Rugby playoffs. Paris was the host this year and not only was Paris the host, France had finally made it all the way to the semi-finals!

Apparently this moment had been a long time in coming. The air was electric.

France won their match over the first weekend. They beat out New Zealand, and it was a coup. Luckily I was stashed away in my apartment in the center of St Germain des Pres. I could hear the game blaring over the loudspeakers in a boisterous bar a few blocks away. And when the moment of triumph came, "La Marseillaise" soared through the air. My view out my front window was a front row seat to the victorious drunkenness that went on down there on the mean streets of Paris, France.

The next week excitement verging on hysteria built toward the next match. It was to be the semi-final game, and for Paris' part, it was France versus Britain. The French were beside themselves. You can imagine. Millions of Englishmen arrived to cheer their boys on, while trying to crowd out the French. Paris was a madhouse. The bridges and metros filled to overflowing. Much loud street scene every night.

This time I wanted to be a part of it. So on Saturday I got the apartment ready. I hauled in a stash of salted butter and sugar bread, my definition of junk food having risen to new heights. Some apricot jam and brioche. A mother lode of chocolate.

I took a long shower and changed into my at-home tatters. Then I turned the comfortable couch so it faced the television. I opened the front windows just enough to let the muffled roar coming up from the streets outside come in and join me.

Then I turned the TV on. At the same moment the neighbor next door turned on his TV. I felt at one with Paris.

This would be the first time I'd actually seen rugby in action. The game started—

Wow!

Turns out rugby is played by real men, see. It looked to me like they were playing football basically, yet they wore no protective gear. No knee pads, no shoulder pads, no mouth guards, no helmets, if you please. Not for these guys. And they were big men. Lots of big men hurling themselves viciously at one another.

Yes, real men. I could see their faces, and good looking they were too. Rugby apparently attracts men with fabulous bone structure.

I could see their hair flying. Such nice long European hair. I could see their rippling muscles, and their tight rear ends. Nothing was hidden in those charming wet-suit uniforms they wore. The French were in blue. The English were in red.

Nothing was hidden under mounds of protective armor. Mouth guards? Don't make me laugh. Their faces were totally visible.

When they kicked the ball, the concentration, indeed ferocity, was visible. They threw themselves into piles, just like American football. They ran up and down this immense field. They ran into one another and heads snapped back and all that, but somehow nobody was seriously injured. Nobody threw themselves at the ref and had a fit. Sometimes a member of one team had to be roughly pulled off a man from the other team, but not often. Not that I saw gentlemen out there. I saw ruthlessness. But it seemed the game went on.

And okay, get this—

There were NO commercial breaks. As in, no rest for the boys, I mean hunks, out there on that field. The game never stopped.

And such men. I was hanging onto my couch reveling in those men. Sweat flying, oh yeah, baby. They were ferocious. Lots of rough play down there on that field. But these players were real people, not those robot monster things we get in American football.

Who knew rugby was so sexy!

The game played without a hitch. Just bull roared right along. An hour or so of nonstop intensity.

I was already looking forward to next week's game. The finals. South Africa was waiting to play either Britain or France. South Africans were even now gathering in Paris to add to the sports hysteria.

I just knew France would win. Because karmically it would be so right. They were the host here. It had been so long for the French to feel this kind of raw earth power. Even they deserve this kind of triumph once in a while—

But they lost.

Suddenly all was silent in the means streets of Paris. No "Marseillaise" blared.

And everyone slunk home to bed.

METRO TICKETS
CHANGE COLOR

Suddenly, out of nowhere, the unknowns in charge changed the color of the metro tickets. The old ones were purple. The new ones were white.

The change had been gradual. For a while one could get either purple or white, and for a while I was on the right side of God, because I got the purple tickets and knew peace.

The black day did come, though, when I was handed a packet of white tickets. Every nerve in my body leapt up. This was not good—

I took them reluctantly. I raised fear-filled eyes to the woman behind the glass. "Oh, they're just fine," the metro person cooed at me. "Perfectly good, Madame. Same as purple tickets."

She was lying. I knew it. She knew it. I still had some purple ones, so I left silently.

The time came when the last purple got used, leaving only white. They were blindingly white, these new tickets. Like little hospitals.

What had been wrong with the purple ones, for god's sake? Why did people constantly tamper with perfectly good things?

I hate change. Especially in Paris. Change is dangerous in Paris, when one's grasp of French is tepid at best, so one cannot complain or rage or even explain oneself when caught in crossfire or needing a reasonable explanation.

The metro stile is a precise machine. It slurps the ticket out of your fingers and spits it out a foot away. One then pulls the ticket out and pushes through the bar thing, attaining, thereby, entry into the underground metro system of Paris.

There are always hordes of people, all in a terrible hurry, rushing up from behind to complete the same transaction. There is a sense of urgency. What if the metro is right there, and someone misses it because of my nonfunctioning white ticket? Would I be able to protect myself from the stampeding herd?

I approached the stile, the day of the first white ticket, with total misgivings. It had begun to seem to me that there were implied dares to get it wrong behind all things public transportation in the City of Light, so I just didn't trust this. I smelled a fish.

I put the ticket in, and it popped right out where it was supposed to, but instead of a nice green light, a hostile red with a big "X" on it lit up. Heart dropped to the ground. Sure enough, when I pushed the bar thing, it refused to budge.

Okay. Not to panic. I had more tickets. I tried two more. The line bursting behind me.

The answer was NO.

Okay then—

Sweat on my forehead, I pushed through the people hovering, hysteria at the holdup barely at bay, and marched back to the info person. It was a long march. It was a man this time.

"The white tickets don't *marche*," I said. He took them

from me, ran them all through a machine of some sort, and handed them back to me. I kept one out and put the rest in my purse. I got through the stile.

But, I didn't trust these tickets. So next time I needed to use the metro I bought another pack, praying for purple. I got purple. I was very happy. These purple tickets would hold me for another couple of days.

Meanwhile, doing due diligence, I Googled to see if there were complaints about white tickets not working. No.

Okay. It was my attitude. So when I ran out of purple, I grimly put the white tickets back in my purse, and set off.

It was an unfamiliar metro station where I needed to experiment with the white ticket. The metro station was in a dirty, businesslike, non-touristy part of town.

I was already on edge. I'd just failed to get into the fan museum I'd been looking forward to, well, getting into. There was a scheduling issue with this fan museum. It was only open to the public three hours a day, three days a week. And to gain entry one had to ring a bell at the door of a large, forbidding building. I had been unable to contend with the disembodied voice babbling in French, coming through the speaker.

So I'd slunk away, and descended back into the bowels of the metro, one failure under my belt.

It was also, by now, even in the metro, rush hour.

The ticket was slurped from my fingers—

The white ticket did not work.

Sh—t. I whirled around and rushed up to the info cage. Totally pissed. This was the last straw. The Sophia Loren lookalike info woman was in a don't-mess-with-me state herself. I didn't care. I shoved my white ticket at her. My French? "These tickets, they does not works," I yelled.

Yeah well, right. She wasn't having any of that. "They do work," she yelled back.

"Non," I said with my best accent. It was all I had. "The white billet isn't works."

"Mais oui, ils marchent," she said, nostrils flaring. She ran them through the same machine the man did the other time. "Here. Use them. The white works."

The stile was right there. It sucked my ticket in. People were all over the place. Nope. Red light. I whirled back, pushing people out of the way. "Not marching, goddammit," I yelled at her. "Goddammit" was in English.

"It works. *Faissez encore,"* she snapped. *"Merde,"* I heard her say to her coworker. Up yours, I thought. I tried again. I heard something click, and I fell through the stile. Did the bitch flip a switch?

I could feel the red and steam and aging lines and faded lipstick and lank hair hanging all over my coat and scarf and black shoes. So I told myself to get it together—

But why? I crumpled a white ticket. The French are totally at one with the pissed-off female.

All the way home I obsessed about lack of fluency in a foreign language. How it was impossible to throw a fit, demand my rights, or better yet an apology for making things so pointlessly difficult. That there was always, always the next hurdle lying in wait—

Like this pointless problem with the idiotic white metro tickets.

My stop arrived. Louvre-Rivoli. Ah. Thank god. A sane place. Like the Baltimore train station after Grand Central in New York.

I went to the info guy there. I was no longer furious, but I was a woman of few words. Literally.

I handed him my white tickets. "They don't work." He did the run through the machine thing again.

"They'll work now," he said. He smiled reassuringly.

It was late. I was tired. I took the tickets and went home. I'd deal with it later. At my door, as I was turning the key, I finally remembered the word for "never." As in *"Ils ne marchent pas JAMAIS."*

Next morning , as I headed out the door for the metro I had a little word with God. "Okay, God," I said, "I don't know how You are going to fix this small issue for me, but see, You're gonna."

I set off.

I got to the metro. I went down the steps and walked down the long underground passageway. My hair was blown to bits as usual. I went down one more flight of stairs. I went up to the stile. I put the white ticket in.

The white ticket did not work.

I turned around. I went back up the first flight of stairs. I walked down the long passageway. My hair again blown to bits, but this time in the right direction. I went up to the man in the info cage. Different man than the one yesterday afternoon.

"The white ticket doesn't work for me." I'd been practicing. My French was at least coherent. "I don't know why they don't work for me, but they don't. Please, I want the violet ones."

He said, *"Mais, c'est impossible, Madame.* The white ones do work."

I had spent time with my French/English dictionary before leaving the apartment. I said, "I am sure the white ones *should* work. But they don't. *Pas pour moi.* Monsieur, it is my vacation, and for my vacation I want calm. I do *not* want a problem with the metro." I tapped the counter severely.

At the tap he did a miniscule double take. He took the tickets and began that run through again. I said wearily, "That has been done already. Twice." I even managed the French inflection for weariness. The French do weary very well. I'd picked it up.

"Deux fois?" He grew thoughtful. He ran one of them through. Then suddenly he was counting my white tickets. Then he counted out the same amount of purple ones. My heart quickened—

He handed me a wad of PURPLE tickets!

I skipped off to the stile. I didn't care that my hair was blown to bits again. I sailed through. Just like the old days. My grin was hurting my cheeks. Thank you, God. Thank you, God. Thank you—

I figured it would be worth it for the rest of the trip to beg for purple in a weary fashion. It would be worth it. My French would certainly improve.

A few days later I blathered about this purple/white war to a few people at the American Church. Jasmine, who was from Ireland, was four months pregnant and had lived in Paris for a year—I'll never forget Jasmine—Jasmine said, "Does your purse have magnets in it?"

Yes, my purse did have magnets in it. The snaps were magnets. "That'll do it," she said. "Desensitizes the strip on the white tickets."

FALLING IN LOVE
IN L'ÉGLISE
SAINT-JULIEN-LE-PAUVRE

I fell in love in L'Église Saint-Julien-le-Pauvre. I was seated in the compact sanctuary of the oldest church in Paris. I was in a soft dream of ancient stone, flickering candlelight, gothic and gold altarpiece, beautifully dressed classical music devotees leaning into the wondrous sounds issuing from the lungs of soprano Edwige Bourdy.

I should have been listening to Mlle. Bourdy sing. She was singing one gorgeous rendition of the Ave Maria after another, and it was for that reason I was there.

But suddenly I caught sight of him. Or rather I caught sight of less than half of his profile. He sat two rows in front of me, on the other side of the aisle. He was tall, blond, and handsome. That is, I assumed he was tall—he had a large head. I was sure he *had* been blond, but now was a distinguished gray/blond. And even though it was only his profile I saw, it was an amazingly handsome profile.

He was avid about the music, which I found totally endearing. Because he was an athletic sort of man, kind of an aging German football player sort of man, who had some-how found his way to St. Julien's on a Saturday night, to sit on fairly uncomfortable chairs, listening to classical music, instead of doing…I don't know, maybe playing cards or hav-ing a rowdy dinner somewhere, or bonding with his teenage sons?

He wasn't alone.

He was with a woman. This woman was his wife. I know a wife when I see one. I envied this woman. She had my man. Although she didn't seem nearly as entranced with him as I was.

On the other side of him sat the couple they had come with. Probably American tourists. I could barely make out the bald pate of the man sitting next to him, but it looked American.

Given the fact that the two men were sitting next to each other, the wives on either side of them, I figured that they were the friends, had been college roommates. Had remained friends through thick and thin, including the two wives, and probably children who had cost them an arm and a leg, but were finally out on their own, so these two couples could now reap the fruits of a life well lived.

Much like I was also, there in Paris, at St. Julien, listen-ing to beautiful music in this baroque atmosphere.

His wife was too thin, and seemed vaguely discontent. Maybe even sad. She appeared just a trifle resigned. To my object of desire? Could it be? Was she bored? Were the two of them bored? With each other, I mean. Not the music and the atmosphere, of course, which were both too perfect for words.

They were obviously well fixed. She had on really hand-some shoes, and she wore slacks, which were quite chic, and just a tad dashing for a Parisian woman her age in this setting. Her hair, which was dark, was well cut, and her profile was as good looking as her husband's. Hers, though, had more the look of an English patrician.

I like the English patrician look—

For a second, my devotion almost swayed in her direction, but he leaned over and, smiling, whispered something to her. The smile drew me right back into his aura. She didn't smile in return.

Poor man, I thought. Making do, best he can. A classic case of the malcontent wife—

I've been one. So I'm not casting aspersions. I simply know of what I speak. Back to my man.

He was doing his bit. He was enjoying the show. He was murmuring to his wife. He was enjoying the atmosphere—

The atmosphere was medieval in modern Paris. I'd already been to three concerts here, from Chopin to a modern-day interpreter of the castrata, singing everything from opera to ballads. I'd missed the New Orleans jazz, to my dismay, until I remembered that I could simply go to New Orleans to hear it, next time I had the urge.

It was an easy metro ride to St. Julien, except for the time I'd rushed over from a meditation meeting. I was late and rushing up the stairs of the metro St. Michael, when I tripped over my pants and fell, luckily uphill. No one paused, for which I was very grateful, but later I saw the bruises, and they impacted my yoga for the next week. Which made me mad.

Everyone in the audience had their coats off, but the effortlessly chic scarves stayed on. It was warm in the church, but it was cold outside, and certainly I'd been afraid the interior would be chill. But no, amazingly enough it was heated.

Yes, I loved these concerts and, until this one, had held my own with the serious audience and remained entranced by the music and the music alone, until tonight…and him.

At intermission everyone stood up, but as I, too, was with someone, I couldn't force my way into their conversation somehow, even if I'd wanted to set protocol aside and act like an American.

The music started again, and I got to stare at his profile for one more hour. Then the affair had to end.

We all stood up, and they passed right in front of me. As they went by he was indeed speaking English to his friend. Of course his accented English was beyond seductive. His face was oh so handsome, and oh so unavailable—

Because his English wife had found him thirty years ago, hooked onto him, and had the sense to stay married no matter what.

Whereas I had impulsively tossed out two husbands. Now she was vaguely unhappy, and perhaps even a trifle bored, whereas I was anything but bored.

But she had him. She had my man.

What can I say? The better woman won?

Oh dear.

JULIET THROWS
THE CELLPHONE

She was huddled against the metro car. She was pouting, as only a French teenager can do. Dark eyes veiled in hauteur. Pout as big as Brigitte Bardot, whom she probably discounted.

He, the equally teenaged amour, was leaning into her. Nuzzling her neck. Murmuring things. Pout. Nuzzle.

Then a half-hearted shove from her, a bit of squirming away.

He—not deterred in the slightest. More nuzzle. More murmur.

More pout.

My mind veered across the ocean—

To Justin and Ashley, hypothetically speaking, in Orange County, California. Same age as Romeo and Juliet here.

They are in a car, not a metro.

She's furious too, just like Juliet, but she's holding him at bay, mainly because she's driving. She's driving because she has the hotter car, a year-old, hand-me-down BMW. Justin drives a truck, which is okay for him, but not for her.

So, Ashley's mad as hell, and Justin is on red alert

because he doesn't know why the hell she's so mad, but he sure as hell knows it's going to get in the way of sex later if he doesn't play it cool and listen up.

Ashley is on a diatribe. A finger-jabbing diatribe. She'd be spitting venom in his face, but she's driving, for which he is grateful. He's basically waiting for her to shut up, so he can apologize. Because it's been twenty-three hours already since they've had sex. If he ever wants to have sex again with her (which he does) he knows how it has to go.

Abject sorrow at his transgression. Promises to never do it again…whatever the hell it is…which is Justin's fatal mistake. He never actually knows what he's done wrong—

Ashley does. And she's told him, over and over.

Things will not go well for Justin in the end, at this rate.

Back to Paris, on the metro.

Juliet was still pouting and squiggling. Romeo was still determinedly nuzzling and murmuring. I was thinking, *Get on with it already.* You two look like idiots. I'm on the side of the Americans in the BMW. At least she *is* raving. This is called communication in my world.

Juliet here—all she was bothering to do was the sultry, I'm-too-languid-to-talk bit, which it is true, men are dazzled by.

And Romeo, all dark wavy hair and scarf, was just doing his job.

Nuzzle nuzzle. Murmur murmur.

Then his cell phone rang, and he (what was he, a moron?) gave it a quick sweep with his eyes just to see, you know. He wasn't going to answer or anything. But just in case it was his best friend Paul, for instance, with some need-to-know info.

Juliet's pouting eyes saw. Her reaction was instantaneous. She went from languid to bitch in one second flat.

She grabbed that expensive cell phone and flung it across the metro car. It landed without hitting anyone, and slid away underneath a seat somewhere.

Romeo's eyes followed it for a split-second…to see where it had landed? Then, without missing a beat, he turned back to his Juliet's neck and began nuzzling and murmuring.

Her languid pout resumed.

CONCERT
AT L'ÉGLISE ST-MERRI

L'Église St-Merri offered free concerts on Saturday evening and Sunday afternoons. I thought these concerts sounded intriguing, and edgy. I should go, right? Since I was attempting to be in touch with the intriguing, edgy me, see, there in Paris, alone, no husband draped around my neck? I should go.

Furthermore, these concerts were described as forums for young musicians to perform their work. Well, I'm as into encouraging young people to develop their creative bones as the next mother of grown children. I know the angst, the suicidal thoughts that come with envisioning perfection, then getting a good look in the mirror, age fifteen.

Hopefully the young musicians to which these concerts referred were older than that—

But it didn't matter. As I said, these concerts sounded edgy. I wanted to check them out. If I was the oldest one there and people were looking at me funny, I'd just laugh hysterically and leave.

I got my map out. I charted the route. I set off, to what I expected to be a twenty-first-century Mozart, performing for free.

It was a sunny Sunday afternoon. I emerged from the metro at the grand Hotel de Ville, where in-line skating lesson were in progress. On the Astroturf set out in the grand space, families lolled with picnic baskets. A real park in Paris mood. I wanted to linger, but I had to get to the church. I had to *find* the church, which wasn't exactly on my map.

I couldn't find the church…

I couldn't believe the church wasn't right where I thought it would be, but fact was, it wasn't. No church.

I pulled out my reading glasses. Pulled out my faithful pocket map of Paris, and rechecked my whereabouts. Several times.

I couldn't find the church. How could it not be here? Churches in Paris aren't shy little chapels. They are huge monsters, and they are all over the place.

I told myself this was psychological blindness because I was over in Les Halles, and I don't like Les Halles. It's an impenetrable maze of dirty streets, dirty buildings, side angles out of nowhere, and confused alleys, some with names, and a lot of young people looking edgy and…never mind.

I wasn't going to quit until I found the *stupide église*. So I circled and circled. Like I said, it was sunny, and now I was hot. I felt like I was lost in New York City somewhere, and no cab would stop—

That happened once, when I was there visiting from Brussels. I was fourteen and very street worthy. But I couldn't get a single cab to stop for me. "Scared of a girl," I hollered after one of them. But that was when Barbra Streisand was actually on Broadway singing in *Funny Girl*. Maybe things were different then. Maybe they just figured I should walk. I was a kid, for chrissake, maybe they thought. Walking wouldn't kill me. So that is what I did. I walked back to my hotel and complained mightily to my father when I got there. He was angry because where the hell had I been, and he'd been worried. It was just one of those days—

So I griped and circled, griped and circled, like forever when suddenly the mystical curtain lifted, and there was St-Merri—

Surrounded by big construction fences barricading the perimeter of the church.

Not even a second of elation was to be experienced, though. Because the massive doors were on the other side of the fences, with no convenient little path through the construction like they had over at St. Suplice. Like maybe the place was closed for the duration.

Merde. I clung to the chain fence, wanting to beat it into submission.

There was *always* this tiny little issue of modern infrastructure maintenance going on, all over the place, in Paris. I broke out into a self-righteous sweat—

One could barely see St. Suplice for the cranes. The incredible toy exhibit at the Musée Decorative? Closed for a massive, months-long cleaning without a word of warning to me. My first apartment was undergoing a government regulated cleaning so that there I was, those first few weeks surrounded by falling rock and insufferable noise, necessitating a most inconvenient move. La Chapelle closing early, apparently for no reason, except that maybe the window-cleaning people got there early and threw a fit about having to do their job under the horrified gaze of three trillion tourists?

I could go on.

Paris was a total pain in the—

But hey, wait a minute. Was that a sign, that small piece

of white paper? There was writing on it. Instantly mollified, I dug for my reading glasses again, and craned in as close as I could to read it.

The sign told me to calm down and get a grip, because the concert was indeed happening and that the way in was a door around to the side, over there.

So I melted. Paris wasn't so bad. In fact, Paris was wonderful. What's a little tension. Tension in and of itself was edgy.

I put my glasses away, and whirled around to go find the promised door, and fell over a small band of elderlies looking for the concert too. They had silently and respectfully stood there watching me read the sign, and now I faced a sea of hopeful faces.

So I reported the good news, waving vaguely in the direction of where I was under the impression the door might be. They all broke into smiles, nodding at each other happily. I waited for them to head off so I could follow them safely into the church.

But they stood there, looking at me. And suddenly I understood. They had made me their leader, and I didn't have the vocabulary to advise them of their mistake.

Please God, show me the damn door.

I set off, and of course, there wasn't a door to be had. I couldn't believe it.

Twice I went around the circumference of the large church, my faithful acolytes following me without protest. Finally, a door I'd seen the first time, but had written off as a mere service door, became the only one to try. It was not what I had had in mind as the entry to an arty and edgy happening.

I hesitated. The five elderlies hesitated too. It was such

an insignificant door, looking like it was never but never used. What if sirens went off? What if the ground opened up and swallowed us? I had a responsibility to my new friends.

But they smiled at me sweetly and encouraged me to take the bold step. They fluttered their hands at me. Go on, they urged.

What was I, for godsake? An American or a mouse? I approached cautiously, gave a careful push, the door swung open, and voila, inside this shadowy and damp edifice sat an audience, waiting quietly.

Ah, sweet victory. My companions and I nodded to each other one more time and went our separate ways.

After a quick perusal, I took a seat.

St-Merri was a vast, dark place. Echoing heights. Wavering light. Thin air. Ghosts lurking.

The audience was murmuring. I wished I had someone to murmur with, because we went on to wait a long time.

But finally a round-bellied man bustled up to the front, puffed up, and began the introduction. I settled back. Ah. At last. Art. *Musique*. So Parisian. *Oui*.

So yes, the potbellied man began speaking. He positively dripped enthusiasm for the work we were about to hear. At least I thought we were about to hear, but no—

The bulbous man went on and on with his introduction. Twenty-five minutes he stood up there, blathering his awe and appreciation for this work, making sure we were given a soupcon of each and every teeny, eeeny nuance. Twenty-five long minutes. I checked.

I didn't understand a word he said. Didn't want to understand a word he had to say. He was obviously ecstatic over his moment in the sun, and not about to relinquish his hold on our attention. Never had an artistic work been given a more thorough intro than this one here. I grew to detest every single thing about this man...and still he oompahed on.

Finally, *finally*, after even the most stoic of Parisian started to cough and shift, a screen rolled down behind him, and as if coming out of a messianic trance, he stopped.

A screen? Good lord, I hoped this wasn't just going to be a video performance. My brow beaded sweat, in spite of the damp.

But no. Thank you, Lord. It was not to be a canned performance, because now, finally another man, a very thin young man, carrying a messy sheath of music, stood up from where he'd been hiding in the audience, and carried his lanky body over to a battered grand piano. He put the music down, loosened his voluminous scarf, and sat down. There was a polite patter of applause, and the pianist began to play. I settled back.

A movie sputtered onto the screen, and that is when I gleaned a tad of what the audience had already been told in excruciating detail.

I was in for a showing of a well-known Russian silent movie called *Cuirassé Potemkine* (who knew?), which was made in 1925 by the famous (I checked in Wikipedia the minute I got home) Russian filmmaker Sergei Einsentein.

My first inkling, there in the church, of what the story was about came when the French subtitles appeared underneath the Russian credits. Underneath the Russian, the French was as clear as English. I saw that I was in for a silent movie about a mutiny on a battleship (yes, the *Potemkine*) in 1905. Having some knowledge of Russian history, I knew I was not in for a happy experience.

With a flourish, the young man began to play. At last—music!

His idea of brilliant music turned out to be banging, roiling, hugely melodramatic music, heavy on the pedal. Which matched what was going on up on the battered screen.

I read later that the original music for the movie had impressive credentials. All very complicated and involving important Russians and things like that, and so the intention could have been to recreate the original showing.

I'll never know.

It was ghastly. It was a harsh, sad, and soon to be ugly story. The grand piano was beaten up by the flying fingers of the emaciated pianist. The screen floated like a limp sheet in the medieval space. The air was soft and damp, just like the huge but gentle old church, and seemed ill equipped to tolerate such a spectacle as Russian mutiny within its walls.

I wanted to run screaming. But it would have been rude to run from such arty edginess, right? So I sat for five more painful minutes trying to give the worthy enterprise a chance.

But no. This was awful, and even God knew it.

So I stood up quietly and slid to the back of the audience. I watched awhile longer. I watched the pianist in his threadbare sweater and cap, and hoped this was a costume for the event. I watched the dutiful audience, although there was now a steady trickle of deserters. I took a photo of candles at the foot of the altar. And the silent movie flickered on in this crumbling, blackening space, the music continuing to break eardrums.

I was turning for the door when I felt a swoosh over my head. I looked around. I stopped. In another minute, another swoosh—

Then I saw the pigeon.

It was trapped in the church. I couldn't even imagine

how he'd gotten in, given my own difficulties in that area. But there he was, flying back and forth, from one stained-glass window to the other. I watched, transfixed.

He didn't fly frantically, but he was perplexed. No way out? He was persistent. Like somehow, if he continued to fly in his stately swoops back and forth across the huge space, he would attain freedom.

I watched the pigeon, so calm and maybe fatalistic in the face of entrapment. I clutched my hands. I wondered if there was a contingency plan for this issue. A special number to call at a special department at fire stations perhaps. Like for cats stuck in trees.

Back and forth the bird flew. Swooping down just enough to be heard over the piano. Up he'd swoop and land on a huge window at the front of the church. In a minute he'd sweep back through the entire length of the church to land on the high window at the other end. A minute there, then back again.

I began to panic for the bird, so—

I left. There was nothing I could do for him. I couldn't bear to watch. His calm in the face of entrapment was majestic.

Outside was a long, dark, bustling alley filled with tourists and locals. The narrow corridor was lined on either side with tiny art galleries. Bicycles whirred by, and I could smell hot apricot croissants.

Maybe the pigeon's calamity might be less than I thought. He was, after all, a Parisian pigeon. Maybe this was a regular occurrence, and he'd be okay. Maybe St-Merri was his home, and he was simply politely registering his opinion of the raucous music happening.

Maybe he was a part of the show? The carefully raised

pet of the pianist, who saw to it the bird ate before he did, hence the pianist's skeletal appearance?

I hastened back to the Hotel de Ville, and sat in the sun watching the in-line skating class. Free pigeons were all over the place. I don't like pigeons—

Until the pigeon in St-Merri.

Maybe that was the edgy part.

LES PARCS DE PARIS

I die for zee parcs in Paris. They are retreats from the noise and history of Paris. They are quiet. Beautifully quiet even when children are playing. It's their mood. Enter and know a moment of peace.

In no particular order, the parks I sat in, rested in, meditated in, snacked in, took photos in, shared with other Parisians. It is a luscious list. A visual way to show the sheer multitude of these gems.

And this is but a tiny spectrum.

Cimetière du Montparnasse
Jardin du Luxembourg
Parc du Champs de Mars
Jardins du Trocadéro
Place des États-Unis
Jardin Catherine Laboure
Square Bouciant (Bon Marche)
Square Récamier
Square Santiago du Chili (La Tour Maubourg metro)
Musée Rodin
Square S. Rousseau (by Basilique Ste Clotilde)
Square G. Pierné (end of Rue de Seine)

Cluny Sorbonne-La Sorbonne Musée Nat.
    du Moyen-age et Cluny
Palais Galliera/Square Brigole Galliera
Parc Monceau
Jardin Ranelagh
Jardin des Serres (greenhouses)
Sq. Louis XVI (near Madeleine)
Jardin Tuileries
Jardin du Carrousel
Jardin du Palais Royal
Square Emile Chautemps
Jardin Anne Frank (Musée d'Art et d'Histoire
    du Judaisme)
Jardin du Musée Carnavalet
Square Charles V Langlois
Place des Vosge
Place Dauphine (Île de la Cité)
Square Jean XXIII (behind Notre Dame)
Promenade Plantée
Jardin des Plantes

And there are more. So many more.
Merci, Paris!

BOYS IN PARIS

I went to the Opera Garnier another time. I saw a ballet called *Les Enfants du Paradis*. It was the story about one to-die-for courtesan (is there any other kind?), the four men (I'd settle for two) who loved her, and the pesky girlfriend of the man the courtesan loved best, who was the mime. The mime madly adored the courtesan of course, except he spent the whole ballet trying to stave off temptation by running away every time she threw herself at him…until the end when—

I won't spoil it.

My seat was wonderful. Natalie had gotten me my seat way down in row five center, while she continued to defy death up there in the rafters.

Down where I was, I first mistook the proper aisle. I climbed over several million people before plopping down in what turned out to be the wrong seat. Much to the consternation of the woman whose husband's seat it was.

I pulled out my tickets, much flustered, to wave them around so someone could help me. This seemed to cause even more consternation in my row.

Then I felt a firm tap on my shoulder from behind. I turned around. A young gentleman, pink cheeked, age fifteen, solemn and impervious, dressed in an impeccable suit, indicated that my correct seat was back there, right next to him.

I crawled my way out of the first aisle and down the one behind me, climbing over my savior. I tried to sit down with a modicum of grace. His self-possession was intimidating, and I wished to try to live up to it. Like how I figured Charlotte Rampling would handle this.

I prepared to attempt to make small talk.

But he never said another word, never moved, never looked anywhere but at the stage.

At the end of the ballet, after the frenzy of applause, the crowd took up a kind of rhythmic clapping, and the men began to call out, clipped and loud, "Bravo."

Suddenly next to me a man's voice boomed, with utter certainty and authority, "Bravo!" This was my young gentleman? I cast a quick look, and yes, it was he. Those round cheeks. Full lips. Long shaggy hair, shining and clean. Booming "bravo" like his esteemed grandfather must have done. I couldn't help it. I grinned at him. "Excellent, *n'est pas?*" He beamed at me. Nodded. Then back to business—

"Bravo."

One day I was taking a shortcut through Parc Monceau. I had stopped to take photos of the statues of the old writers and their adoring muses (so I could show those back home what I was complaining about), when this exuberant six-year-old bounced up behind me and shook my purse to get my attention. He was wearing a Superman costume.

"Do you like my cape?" he asked. He was sputtering with joie de vivre. "This costume is a present to me, and one day I am going to fly straight into the sky up there." He twirled his red cape and flung his arms to the sky. I tried to murmur appropriate things back in a clear enough accent so as not to scare him away.

"My mother…Maman loves Batman," he babbled. "But I tell her that Superman is better." I clucked my agreement with him, and smiled at his Papa, who was standing off to one side. "Yes," he said, voice high with delight, "Superman is sooo much better," and then he ran off.

One time at the Garnier in the daytime, I stood on the balcony taking pictures. There was a brother and sister out there with me. She was about twelve, and was trying to get something out of her backpack, which her older brother, about fourteen, was holding for her. They were tourists too, and were muttering in German to each other. He was determined to rise above his impatience. She, oblivious to it.

She searched and searched. Finally, impatience won out. He abruptly dropped the backpack. The little sister was taken aback. I caught her eyes and shrugged. Brothers, what can you do?

She smiled. He saw. As I walked toward the door to go back in, he stepped over to open it for me. "She was taking just a little too long," he said in perfect English, his German accent just a trace. He bowed me through the door.

I love Jacques Lartigue's photographs of a Paris in days gone by. Having seen his photos of little youths wearing high-button shoes and straw boater hats and sailor suits having a fab time sailing boats in the pool and fountain at the Luxembourg Gardens, I hastened over, camera in hand, to witness the charming sight.

They sail boats the old-fashioned way. That is to say without engine and remote control. They use a stick. The boats are large and feature sails.

But, *quel dommage*. It is a tedious affair.

Young Philippe was there with his adored granny, but even she couldn't make this business worth it.

I watched. All these parents and grandparents were leaning over their comatose children, gleefully putting the boat in the water, then handing the stick to their kid.

It was just a stick, for godsake. What was the kid supposed to do with it?

Give the boat a bit of a shove, that's what, and voila, one had a boat in movement.

Philippe's grandmother had to do the stick bit too. Philippe just didn't want to get the hang of it. He seemed polite. He wore glasses, so one assumes he was the polite sort, or maybe even a little passive aggressive. It can't be easy being a kid who wears glasses—

But so she pushed the boat, and out it moved into the middle of the pool. Philippe clutched his head as Granny triumphantly cheered the boat on.

All the parents' boats had moved into the middle of the pool. All the parents were cheering.

This is when it could be read plain as day on Philippe's face, and the rest of the kids' faces too, that a remote control and some buttons to push would have made the whole event so much more bearable.

HEAD FIRST

One day, emerging from the metro like a sprig from the dark earth in spring, the sun having been high in the sky when I went down, rain poured down on my unprotected head. Before I had time to yell "Help," everyone else had their umbrellas up.

This is when it hit me, the state of vulnerability I was in every time I climbed the stairs up to street level.

Head first is not the usual mode of entry. Only when one is born, or is diving into a pool, does the head carry the weight of discovery.

Suddenly the fact that I was emerging into the unknown eight million times a day head first crashed down on my naked, vulnerable, metro-emerging psyche, and I ducked from the rain and tripped over the teenager in front of me.

Until that moment, I'd kept issues with the metro at bay. Which was difficult. My style is to nitpick to death anything I have to do over and over and over again.

I'd managed to ignore the hordes of people who used the metro, like all the time. Especially while negotiating the stairs, of which there were many. The stairs are wide but steep. The escalators are painfully narrow. Both are always teeming with people.

People hobbling up or hobbling down. People carrying suitcases and strollers, couples negotiating the climb or descent ensnared in each other's arms.

There are people who read while ascending or descending. This crew is flat-out looking for trouble. There are codependents calling anxiously to the person traveling with them.

The grim professional bunch, blank faced and focused, are getting their tickets out early, rushing faster if they see/ hear a train pulling into their station, looking through their purses or briefcases, talking on their BlackBerrys—

It's an austere Parisian mayhem.

Maybe this is why I never noticed my head always emerged first.

So, on this day when I finally noticed my head was a target for god knew what awaiting me at the top, I stopped, red flags ripping the air out of the sky.

My bare head would take the hit—from weather, traffic, gunmen/women, irate wind chill factor, mob scenes, or the end of the world even—

One time I'd emerged into a parade of demonstrators. One time it was a mother losing an argument with her baby's stroller. Many times it was simply the wrong place entirely.

Whatever was waiting up there, my head got it first. I was off kilter anyway, because whatever I found up there, it wasn't the world as I knew it. It was Paris. I was a Californian who never but never went underground, let alone on foot, let alone needing to contend with weather factors that might be hostile, and for which we are chronically unprepared.

I did have my umbrella that day. I had my umbrella every day. I'm no fool. I fumbled and got it up as the rain reached me—

Or rather, as my head reached the rain.

Furthermore, on this emerging head first issue, one emerged into the mass of people who had stayed on top of the world, the ones who eschewed the metro and took busses or cabs or their own car, or walked. Thereby keeping their own heads safe.

Does this state of affairs play subliminal mischief with the psyche of the metro-riding Parisian? In fact the metro-riding anyone, including New Yorkers, poor darlings?

At least in car-bound worlds (like California) one is on top of things, not below the radar, as it were.

Or are we? What we are, actually, is trapped in our cars, witnessing first hand, traffic lights turning red more often than they do green. There are traffic standstills on freeways. There is the never-ending roadwork and the accompanying detours—

We are victims, in car-bound worlds.

So that, even though emerging from the metro in the vulnerable head-first position, one is still mobile, still free to come and go. One is in a state of forward motion, even though one may be about to have one's block knocked off.

What about the descent? Is there a feeling of jumping off a cliff? The descent associated with hell? The descent into the socially unacceptable "bottom"?

But this is immediately corrected on the other end. One gets back into the fray head first, eager and fearless.

Maybe this descending and ascending, day in and day out, is a powerful tool. Subliminally imparting the message that one is strong, fearless, brave, and free.

So that using the metro is a life-enhancing practice.

This, then, is a good thing.

BIKRAM YOGA IN PARIS

So a friend of my sister-in-law who was in Paris the same time as I was e-mailed me. "I've been doing Bikram yoga while I'm here. Do you want to join me?"

Every guilty bone in my body shivered. The gig was up—

Yoga had finally joined me in Paris.

Yoga is my soul mate. My yoga practice is my better half, my best self, my nicest self. But yoga is also my main exercise, and I believe in leaving the exercise program at home when I travel.

And so it had gone on my first two trips to Paris. Aside from the small amount of yoga I did in the apartment, there was no yoga. No seeking out interesting yoga studios. I'd Googled both Ashtanga and Iyengar, and yes sir, there was plenty to be had in Paris. Interesting studios falling out of my ears if I had so chosen. Plenty of classes in English. Good way to meet people. But I was on sabbatical from my real life. Besides, I climbed stairs. I walked. It would have to be enough—

And it was.

But now this so-called friend of my sister-in-law, whom I'd met exactly once, had tossed me this unwanted challenge.

I paced the apartment. Why had she done this to me? Didn't I have more than enough still to do, even though this was my third trip?

But maybe this was supposed to be happening. It was my third trip after all. Maybe it was time to take on a more formidable domestic challenge than finding Comet at the grocery store, or mailing my overseas ballot back to the States in time to be counted.

There was one issue though—

"But umm...*Bikram* yoga?" I e-mailed back.

Because that was a bit of a moral dilemma. I did not do Bikram yoga, under any circumstances. Bikram yoga has a bit of a...reputation, what can I say. It is the hot yoga. Where they heat the room up eight million degrees, give or take a degree or two. We snobs over at Ashtanga get that hot without the artificial heat. We snobs over at Iyengar know they don't get the alignment right.

Gym persons, on the other hand, love Bikram. They sweat like hogs and tell themselves this is what yoga is all about. But gym persons' hearts are not really into yoga, now are they?

And finally, Bikram is a famously successful franchise. I mean, how totally non-yogic is a successful franchise? I rest my case.

But I was starting to think yoga in Paris might be interesting. Not Bikram, of course. But maybe Iyengar? I certainly wasn't up to French Ashtanga. Yes, maybe nice, safe, traditional Iyengar—

"It was so hot, the teacher, Andre, wore this teeny thong," e-mailed the friend of my sister-in-law.

It was a trek to get there. First there was the six-block walk to the metro—

A mini adventure, see. Much dashing in front of slower pedestrians, much feeling the speeder faster than me breathing down my neck. The quick jig into the street to get around the mother and baby carriage traffic jam. The smell of coffee. The boulangerie filled with fresh croissants and brioches and sugar bread. Roasted chickens already cut in half in their heated carts. A quick glance at the headlines as I sailed by the kiosk. A quick glance in the window of my latest favorite store to make sure the black jacket I couldn't quite bring myself to buy was still there—

Trying not to get nervous about attempting Bikram in Paris.

Then those two metros and annihilated hair to get downtown, getting off at Hotel de Ville, and then another six-block walk down even more crowded sidewalks, going by a large American-style gym, looking incongruous set amidst the old buildings. Then a right turn at a small alley. Across from the loud, oh so loud Pompidou Center, and there it was— Bikram of Paris.

I had to come all the way to Paris to finally break down and try Bikram.

I felt sick, standing in the line to sign in. Scared. No one ever said Bikram was for crybabies.

The two sweet girls behind the desk were chirping away in English, but all I wanted to do was flee. Everyone appeared to be fourteen. I did not need yoga here in Paris. This was ghastly. I was an idiot, a people pleaser of the worst kind. I barely knew my sister-in-law's friend. I wasn't even sure I would recognize her. Forget it. I was out of here. I was so out of here.

"Ruth? You made it!"

Merde.

She'd told me I'd be soaked when class was over. I could figure that one out. But, she told me, I would need, therefore, to take a shower after class. For the trek home. This was not good, okay? On so many levels. Not the least being taking a shower with a bunch of fawnlike sixteen-year-old Parisians—

Get a grip. I would not be the star of the show anyway. No one gave a damn about…well, anyone but themselves. Besides, I'd be lucky if I survived long enough to take a shower with a bunch of fawnlike sixteen-year-old Parisians. I'd be counting my blessings if I were to find myself stripping bare in Paris—

Hell, I'd been to boarding school. I'd given birth. There's nothing more raw than giving birth—

I could do this.

And I didn't have to do this ever again. That was a promise.

Okay. Proceed.

I pushed open the door to the studio itself very slowly. I wasn't sure how the heat would hit. I'd heard all kinds of rumors, from both aficionados to those who hated it without ever having been. I stepped in very carefully.

The heat almost knocked me flat. It enveloped me like an airless cloud. My forehead beaded up instantly. The acrid odor was somewhat familiar to me. I had spent so much time doing Ashtanga. Heat purifies sweat, is my mantra. But this heat was already in place, not generated by the class. It was deeper, more sucking than even the heat in Florida in July. That heat had scared me, and I'd been afraid to leave the house the first week I lived there. But that was pre-yoga.

Okay, so here was the heat and it was weird. Somehow

benign, though. I felt the instant calm I always feel upon entering a studio for yoga.

The studio was small. People were already there. Only two rows. It was reassuringly dim. I laid down my mat and carefully sat down, then lay down. I didn't want to overdo anything at all before we got started on what I was sure was going to be a killer series of postures I wouldn't be able to handle.

I was at the bottom of a well, in an Amazon rain forest, in the middle of Northern European Paris. But this was, ultimately, yoga, right?

I would survive. I'd move slowly. I'd use my ujai breathing to keep me centered.

I wore the one pair of yoga pants I'd brought. They were full length, but I could see that skimpy shorts in honor of the heat were the preferred choice. Even on those with bodies that were, shall I say, large. At the sight of those bodies, I felt a small tinge of hope. If they could survive the heat without keeling over, then hopefully, so could I.

Class started with a brusque clap of the hands, and bright lights slamming on. Blinking in the glare (how non-yogic, right?), I wobbled to my feet, and faced a mirror (also non-yogic). The other new person and I were informed we were not under any circumstances to leave once class started. If we found ourselves in distress, we were to simply and quietly sit down. I cast a look of longing at the closed door—

And class began. There was never another chance to stare at the door. I bucked up, rolled with the punches, and commenced to do the best I could.

It was totally different than any yoga I had ever done. It felt like a cross between calisthenics and yoga, or like a cross between the military and yoga. The commands were crisp and precise, but spoken in the accented English that made all the bossiness sound very Audrey Hepburn. There was always the abrupt, no-nonsense clap of the hands signaling the start of the next posture.

First half seemed to be all standing balancing poses, not my strong point. The second half consisted of being folded in half on our knees, head to the floor. The fear of choking seemed very real as our heads were told to go down, go down, go down more than that.

Fear of fainting defined the experience. I told myself I was at one with the Serengeti heat, that I would *not* faint, and that if I got out of there without having fainted, I could do whatever I wanted for the rest of my life.

Finally, thank you God, the class did end. I was soaked from head to toe. I was adding my own personal sweat to the room. An unadulterated bliss now defined the experience. I lay there in Shavasana and dreamed of heaven.

Everyone rushed off—much too busy for Shavasana—for their showers. Maybe they all had to rush back to work. Well, I didn't. So I would lie in stillness and heat for as long as I thought I could get away with it, and maybe by the time I got there, the cramped basement locker room would be empty.

Far from it, thank you very much. The place was packed and very, very wet. Looked like a steam room. Felt like a sauna. Apparently Parisian Bikram people take their time showering after class. So I felt a small moment of panic when I contemplated what it was going to take to get street worthy in this dungeon, with absolutely no privacy, except for the few minutes you were in the actual shower.

Luckily the sedative effects of a strong yoga workout were in place too, so I just set to it.

I stripped in the shower. The shower ran for one minute, then turned off. So I had to keep jabbing it back on. It was so hot (I'm not complaining) I emerged with steam coming off my body. Sweating profusely, I reached around several babbling girls to get my clothes and find a place to actually do something about putting them on. It wasn't easy locating a free spot. It wasn't easy to encourage a nineteen-year-old, engaged in intense conversation with another nineteen-year-old, already fully clothed, to relinquish her spot on the bench, thereby making room for me. I did get the girl to move, ultimately, despite being wrapped in a tiny towel, despite having been mauled in class.

Getting dressed wasn't easy. It wasn't easy to dry off… it wasn't possible to actually get dry. It wasn't easy to pull my clothes on over hot, damp skin. It wasn't easy to pack the wet clothes away. It wasn't easy—

But eventually I was able to stagger out to the large grooming area, I guess you'd call it, open to men and women. There were two blowdryers and one mirror, in front of which sat Matilde and Suzette and Agnes, applying their eye makeup *avec tres beaucoup* precision.

So I applied my lipstick with *tres beaucoup* precision. I blew my hair dry completely. I gathered my battered self together, slung my scarf with what energy I had left, crawled back upstairs, bought a vitamin drink for the journey home, assured the sweet girls behind the counter that I had loved it, absolutely LOVED IT…and wobbled out into the madness that is a Parisian sidewalk around lunchtime.

I did love it. Okay, not love. But I respected the physical work I'd done. And I'd loved the heat and the sweat.

I went back. A lot.

LES MUSÉES DE PARIS

There are many museums in Paris. However, I am not a museum lover. My excuse for this cultural transgression is that growing up I was dragged to every museum in the world.

Which is why I am *tres* yawning and dulled and *un petit* how you say BORED OUT OF MY MIND by zee museums filled with all zee leetle tiny *objets de* boringness. And where one is required to be *tres, tres* quiet and only whisper and no laughing please. Absolutely no making fun or laughing—

It's constrained in a museum. They are serious places indeed. Related to history, art, culture, architectural detail nonpareil, all that quiet whispering, guards at every door, can I use my camera or not, am I being crass by even taking pictures instead of standing in worshipful silence, staring at whatever priceless, terribly important item I am staring at—

Thinking how long do I need to stare? Is one minute long enough for this painting? I can see it's a painting from a very long time ago of a serious woman holding a baby who probably died young, and I hate it when that happens, so, maybe I can just move along to the next one…or even fast forward to the front door and outta here—

"Wait a minute," says my companion. "We've only been here for five minutes. You said you'd give me twenty."

It's much better if I go to a museum alone…and the only place that happens is in Paris, where, yes, *I love les musées*.

I die of love for *les musées* in Paris, in fact. But I was choosy, carefully avoiding the monsters like, for instance, the Louvre. I had been there when I was twelve, and had not been impressed with the experience. The Mona Lisa was too small. We seemed to walk miles to even find her. What was up with that? I complained mightily to my mother, but I recall she remained serene in spite of it all.

I didn't go to the clown-like Pompidou, although I do hear good things about what is within.

And I never bothered with the Grand Palais, mainly because the luscious Petit Palais was just across the street.

I went smaller. I went to the Musée de la Poupée. I went to the Galerie-Musée Baccarat, Musée Marmottan, the Musée Nissim de Camondo, the Musée Carnavalet, Cognacq-Jay, Picasso, Rodin, le Petit Palais, le Musée Gustave Moreau, and the Musée de la Vie Romantique. The Musée Jacquemart-André. Also the ones that called themselves Foundations, like Le Corbusier and Dubuffet.

There is a never-ending supply of these small museums.

I liked them housed in what were beautiful private mansions. I liked them if they were quirky and odd or, better yet, hidden. The first trip I was afraid of the hidden ones, but the next year I broke the noose and found Le Corbusier. I even rang the buzzer at Dubuffet.

I liked hunting them down. I got all over Paris this way. That was a huge aspect of museum-going that was so fabulous in Paris. I didn't have to drive to them. I didn't have to sit in a backup on the freeway. I didn't have to stop for gas. I didn't have to sweat parking—Paris is a dream that way.

The Doll Museum was practically behind Bikram Yoga, off of rue Beaubourg, on the outer edges of Le Marais. Quite hidden. I walked up a narrow alley. There was a large park to my right, which turned out to be the back of the Musée d'Art et d'Histoire du Judiasme. I kept walking and there it was, The Doll Museum, attached to the back of a large building. It looked like a lean-to cottage. There was a path with flowers leading to the gate. I could have almost been in Colonial Village in middle Massachusetts.

But I approached cautiously. I wasn't at all sure the *musée* would even be open. There is a seemingly quixotic plan in Paris to keep one on edge as to which museums are open or not on Monday and Tuesday. Some are. Some aren't. Either day. No rhyme or reason. Usually to be safe, to spare myself massive disappointment, I never even considered picking a museum to go to on Monday or Tuesday. But today was Tuesday, a Bikram day. Just by luck I'd spotted a little box on the map called Doll Museum. I love dolls. This was an instant must-see. And it was just up the street from Bikram. So I chanced the Tuesday/museum open or closed issue.

After approaching it diffidently, with no American swagger (god forbid I give a closed *musée* a chance to turn me down), the place was open. The door was easy to open (praise the lord), and the lady inside selling the tickets was easy to understand. What was not to love?

Especially as the cache inside was dolls, glorious dolls, hopefully trillions of them.

It was compact, and turned out to consist of four rooms with all four walls set with panoramas of dolls behind glass.

These panoramas were the ultimate in doll lovers' fantasies. A cornucopia of dolls and their accoutrements. They were arranged in activities, much like the fabulous toy display in the Musée des Arts Decoratifs. It was a fairyland for the likes of a doll lover like me.

Helped by the sedative effect of an hour and a half of yoga, I puttered through the rooms in a state of pure wonderment. So many dolls. So much fantasy. I savored every doll, every bonnet, every laced-up pair of shoes, every miniature tea set.

When I walked in, there were two young women hovered over by a corner of one of the panoramas in the first room. They had backpacks slung over their shoulders. They were murmuring quietly to themselves, but after a bit they fell silent, and just hung over this one corner.

I circled the room slowly, quelling irritation that they were there in the first place, waiting for them to get a move on. They seemed to be making notes. An art school assignment? A very complicated, demanding one—therefore, an infinite amount of time over in this one corner. Stuck like glue in this one and only corner.

In the end, I moved into the next room without having seen that corner. But it wouldn't matter in the end. I'd take my time and catch that one corner on my way out—

Because I didn't want to miss a drop. The dolls were beautiful. They were charismatic. I was drooling.

I made my way around slowly, congratulating myself on not rushing through at my usual museum pace. The rooms were arranged in a circle. So I eventually returned to the first. A good hour had gone by.

The two girls were still there, in that exact same corner…

What the—? C'mon. Enough already. Get over yourselves. You're hogging that corner, did you know that?

What the—?

Drugs, I thought. What else could it be? Maybe I should call an ambulance, in case they were on a bad trip and were too freaked to move.

But pot, most likely. They had that too stoned to realize they had stared at the same doll for an hour feel to them. I considered going up to them and leading them to a different spot. They'd never know. Maybe they'd vaguely note that something was different, but god, it was all so fabulously interesting that nothing else mattered—

Including the American tourist who wanted their spot.

I kept meaning to go back there to see the missing corner. But seriously, what would I have done if the girls were still there, as was obviously a total possibility?

THE PET FLY

There is one major problem with Paris. I am without pet.

Upon arriving back to the apartment there is no pet waiting anxiously at the door or, in the case of my most elderly cat, curled asleep atop of clean laundry. At night there is no thump as the cat arrives in bed.

I sleep alone in Paris, as a result of having no pet.

There is no hissing between cats. No plaintive meow hoping for a treat. No one to which to give a treat.

In the apartment when I am talking out loud to myself, I really am talking out loud to myself. No pets even pretending they understand and sympathize with every word.

No small animals chasing after each other. There is no one moving in my apartment but me. There is no one breathing but me.

There's no one wanting my attention in the apartment. No one sitting on the computer, throwing up, refusing to eat their food.

There is no reason to have a litter box—

There is no odor whatsoever in the apartment but me.

There is no one to say good-bye to when I leave for the day.

There is no one to scold, chase after, clean up after, but…me.

It gets lonely in my apartment with no pets.

Three days before I was to leave to go back to America on my first trip, a fly somehow got into the apartment, which was on the inner courtyard, five stories up. I have no idea where it could have come from, because as it was, I could barely see the sky. I could see the top tip of the Eiffel Tower from the bedroom window, but still the fly wouldn't have come from that direction.

I was not happy to see the fly. I don't like flies. Germy little suckers. So their arrival means I have to kill them, at which I am very good. But it's like a peaceable man who has to put up his dukes to some bully just because he's been challenged. Just because I'm good at tracking down and killing flies doesn't mean I want to do it.

I was totally not into killing this Parisian fly. I was in mourning, for one, that it was time to go home. And secondly, I was in too beatific a state of mind to do anything so drastic as to kill a fly.

Still, I don't like to share my abode with flies, so in this case, after shooing him out didn't work, I left both the kitchen windows open (where I found him), and the two big windows in the living room open. I figured he got in that way. He would find his way out.

He didn't find his way out.

The first night I went to bed vaguely worried he was going to buzz around my head. But he didn't. He was simply there the next morning when I got up, waiting for me in the kitchen. We had coffee together. Then I left, leaving the windows ajar.

He was there waiting, when I got home. In fact he must have been sleeping all day, because he buzzed all over the kitchen while I got dinner together.

Well, hey. I could go there. The fly became my pet. And made my last two days a little happier because when I came home I could share my day with him. I could tell him how unhappy I was to be going.

I did worry he wasn't getting any nourishment…but then maybe he was. Maybe he was leaving during the day like I did, in his case to check out the various Dumpsters, and then was returning in time to spend the evening, just us two.

I was also worried that I'd get up one morning and find his carcass upside down on the kitchen counter. By now I was fond of the little guy. I was relieved, in fact, because here at last was my very own living animal sharing my life in Paris with me.

My last morning in Paris dawned. I could take it slow because I was returning to les États-Unis on an afternoon flight.

The fly was waiting when I came out into the kitchen to make my coffee. I was gloomy, and he could tell. His flying was particularly acrobatic that morning. Maybe he was in the death throes, but I chose to see it as he was trying to cheer me up.

I began to pack, and then decided that this morning I would treat myself to some luscious *tartes*. So I went out to my favorite boulangerie and bought the queen of croissants, the almond croissant. And just because, I also bought the beyond bodacious rhubarb and cream *tarte*.

I set them out on the counter. I intended to snack on them throughout the course of the morning. I had a bite of the rhubarb. Oh my god, nirvana! I took a bite of the almond croissant. To die for.

Then I went back to the bedroom for some more packing.

Packing is arduous. Particularly after six weeks in a place. There is much sorting out. What goes. What gets thrown out. Putting the apartment back exactly as I found it. And so on.

Time slipped by, and with a start I remembered my luscious treats in the kitchen. I dropped a pile of shirts onto the bed, and hastened out.

At first I thought I was in the wrong kitchen. Because there in the kitchen was a fly. Surely not *my* fly, because this fly looked like an ordinary fly. This was a common house pest fly with no charm, no willingness to please or to do the right thing, as my fly had always done, because this fly was actually face first in the middle of my rhubarb *tarte*. His feet and whiskers and grimy little hands, or whatever the hell those creatures consist of, were in feverish motion as he tried to eat his way through the *tartes*. My last-day-in-Paris treat. There was this monster destroying my *tartes* like he had every right.

He didn't hear me coming, so lost in ecstasy was this fly. He didn't stand a chance.

WHAM. Down came my bare hand and smashed that hellish creature before it even had a chance to swallow that last bite.

I never saw my own fly again. Either he saw what I had done to one of his kind, or he had left for the day, and would be terribly disappointed when he got back that night to see the American lady had left…for good.

Or the one I killed was indeed my fly, in which case—

May we meet again under less fraught circumstances.

THE BLACK SHOES

I held them in my arms tenderly, like a newborn baby. I murmured sweet nothings. I got into the elevator and rode down to the courtyard. I walked to the large trash bins and took the lid off the one least full, took a deep breath, murmured one more dulcet coo, then I did it. I let go. I threw The Black Shoes away.

This was at the end of my first trip. These were a pair of rubber-soled black loafer-styled shoes, which ultimately, after one or two tries with my other shoes, I wore every single day.

They served me well. In them, my feet looked totally Parisian. If I wore my Nikes, I was just an American tourist, in Paris for a week, tops. If I wore my brown suede boots, my feet were mangled for days.

If I wore the rubber-soled Black Shoes, I was at one with the other feet in Paris. Although still obviously an American, I fit in. On the metro my shoes sat on the floor comfortable in the knowledge that they looked right at home. In the grocery store, going to the post office, the drycleaners, standing in line at the Monoprix, the Black Shoes made it all so much easier.

Those shoes (brand-new for the trip, and nothing I would

dream of wearing at home) went from needing to be broken in, to slowly but surely becoming the most comfortable shoes I have ever worn.

They gave me and my clothes total confidence. They didn't slip on the wet cobblestones. They didn't show dirt. They looked French. They looked both chic and matronly.

They were my most basic ticket to assimilation. My shoes never let me down.

But the time had come. They had done their duty without faltering, without complaint, without fatigue.

They were frayed around the edges, looking pale and yes, exhausted. The stitching was coming loose.

Never had I had a pair of shoes I wore every day for six weeks. Never had I had a pair of shoes that had done so much walking, climbing, trudging.

But they were worn out. This trip had almost been more than they could handle—

And the suitcases were full to bursting.

The lid of the smaller Dumpster slipped from my grasp after I dropped the Black Shoes in and thudded shut.

Thank you, Black Shoes.

And so—

I am suddenly back home. Azure skies replace pale blue ones. The ocean sparkles like shattered diamonds, replacing the pewter-colored verve of the Seine. People are smiling, getting in and out of big shiny cars. Meanwhile, I know back in Paris the metro is filled to the brim with Parisians wearing their intricate scarves and belted coats, and someone is playing the "Mapleleaf Rag" on the accordion.

California is beautiful, charming, and open. Paris is indolent and elegant with the weight of history adding gravitas to everyday life.

It seems I get to live with both, so I won't cry and sulk. But culture shock is hovering, so I wheedle my way back into the good graces of my cats, and they finally let me kiss them. I unpack slowly.

I want to mourn Paris, but I know she's there waiting. In the meantime, the sun is out here at home. I can hear the waves. Yes, I am very happy to see my car. I go out and check on the blue driftwood.

It still leans on the palm tree. It's always been fragile, so I dab a little more paint on it every year to shore it up. Last summer this activity was of great interest to the little boy next door. He never said anything at all about crafts. He just said, "I think the stick likes it." I beamed at him.

"Can I try?" he said.

I handed him the brush. I held the ladder when he painted the top. He was thrilled. "I made it look better," he said.

You sure did, kid.

And hey, I love you, blue driftwood.

Because of that emaciated twig of driftwood, I discovered Paris and fell in love. I found a new passion when I didn't even know I was looking.

One never knows when inspiration will strike. Inspiration happens in a flash, so pay attention. And then?

Go with it. Immediately.